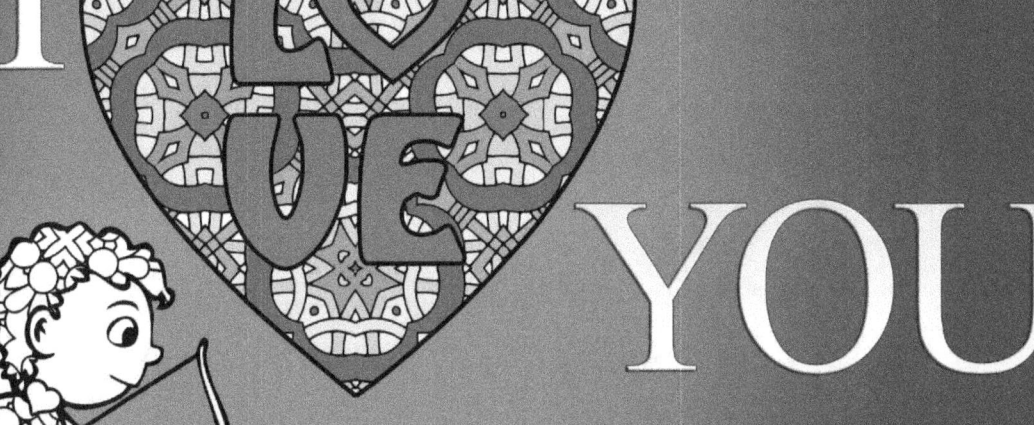

I ❤ YOU IN COLOR

VOLUME 1

Valentine's Coloring Book

Nieves Marqués

Say it with flowers. Say it with a ring...
but this coloring

book is something you are going to
remember

forever.

With this coloring book you are going to
reduce

stress and make your life happier.

You got hearts, bears and cupid, of
course.

You also have love phrases.

Visit
http://www.creatudiariosecreto.com/vale
ntines

to have 5 exclusive pages to download
and print.

Acknowledgment

I would like to thank my family.

Coloring Tips

Just enjoy.

Sharpen your pencil regularly.

Always test any markers or gel pens you use on
a page in the back.

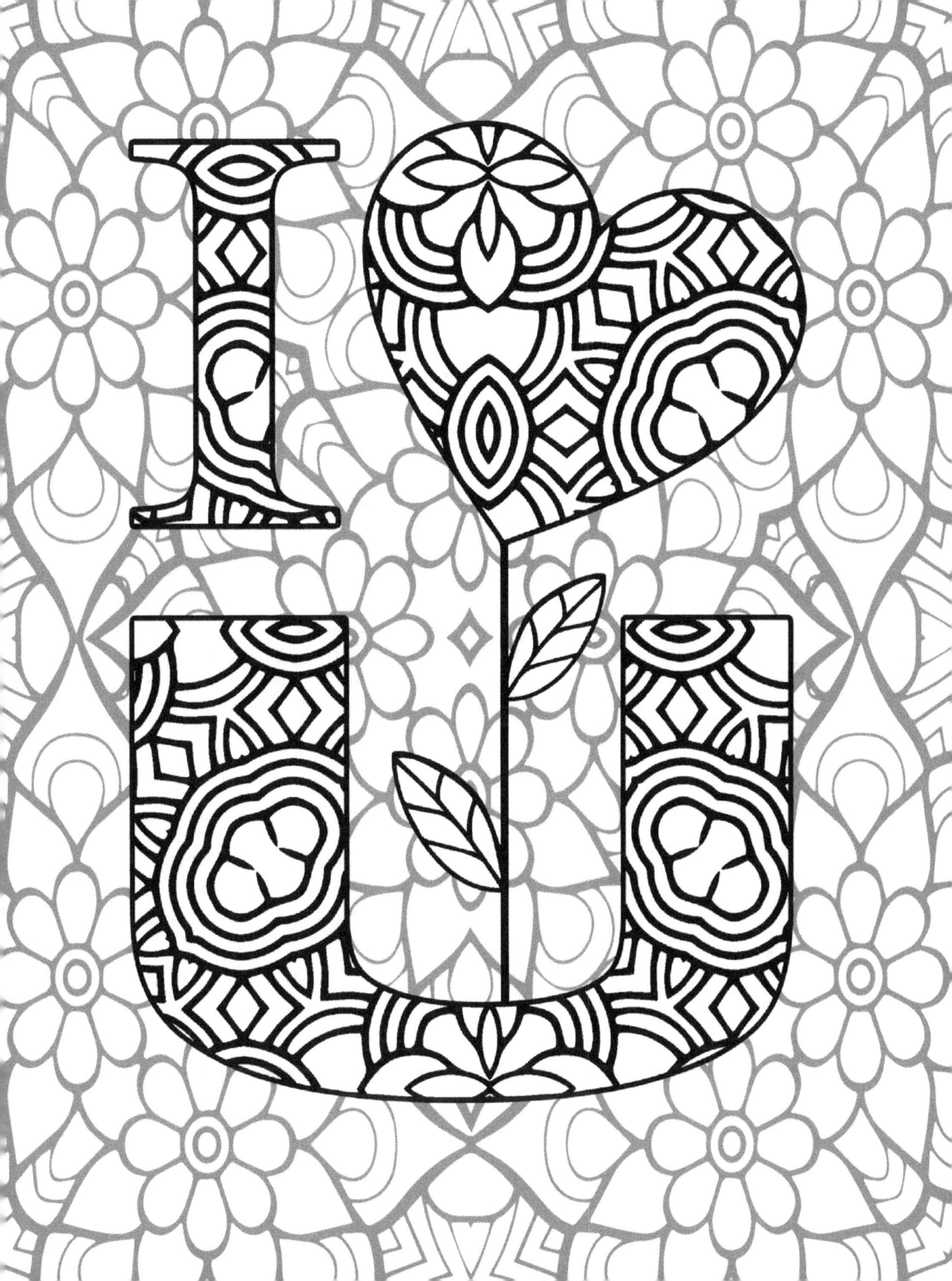

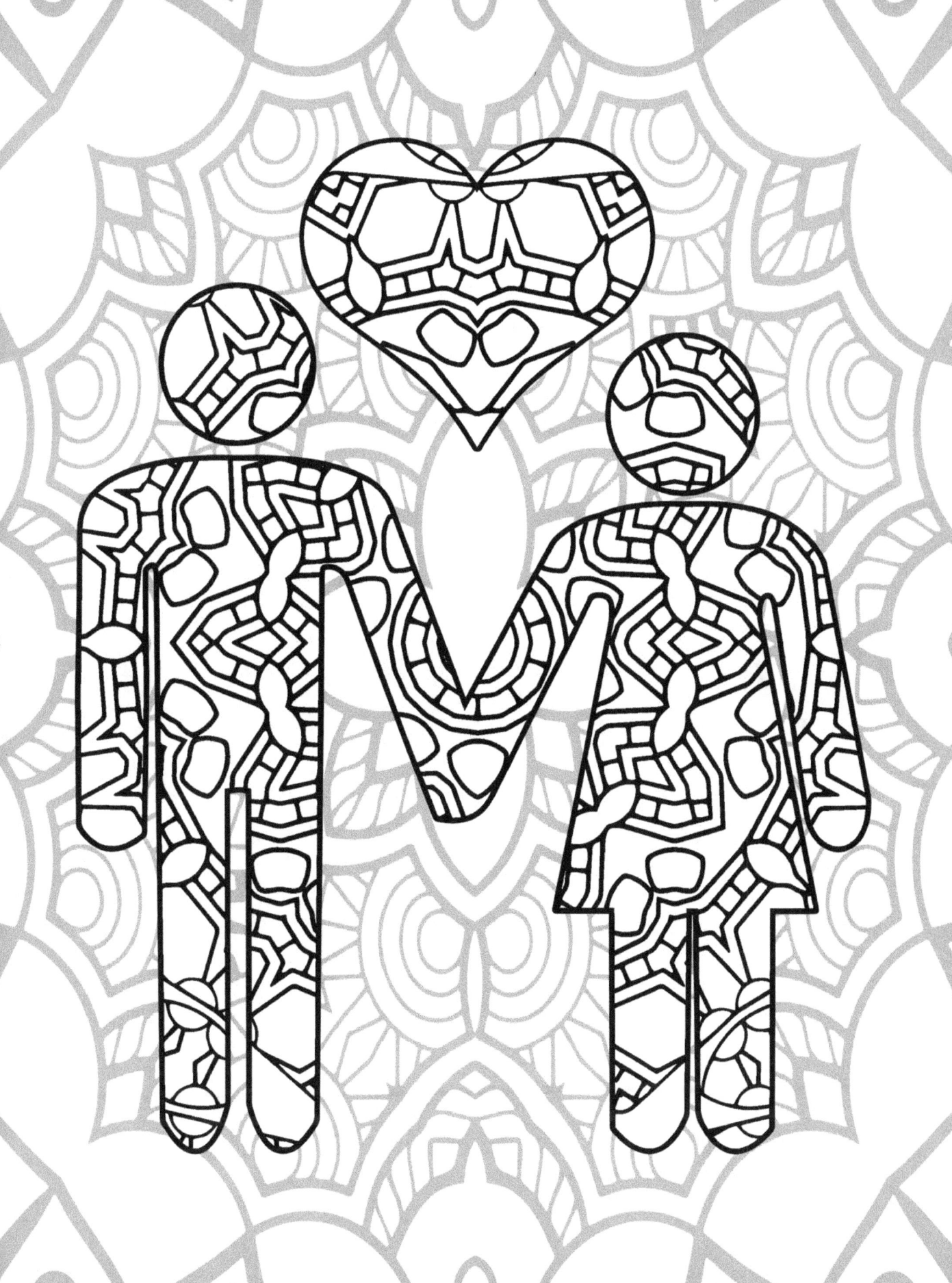

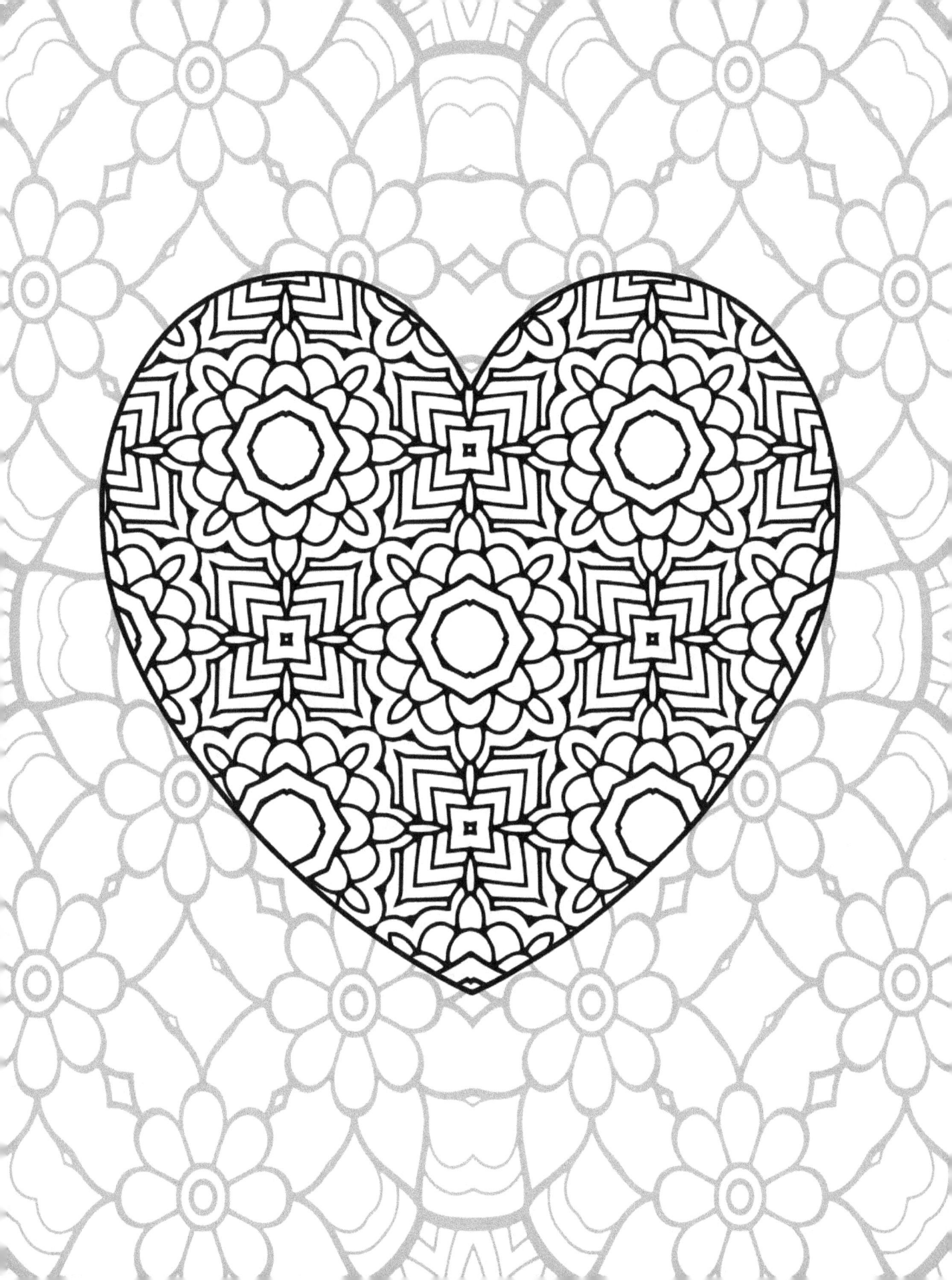

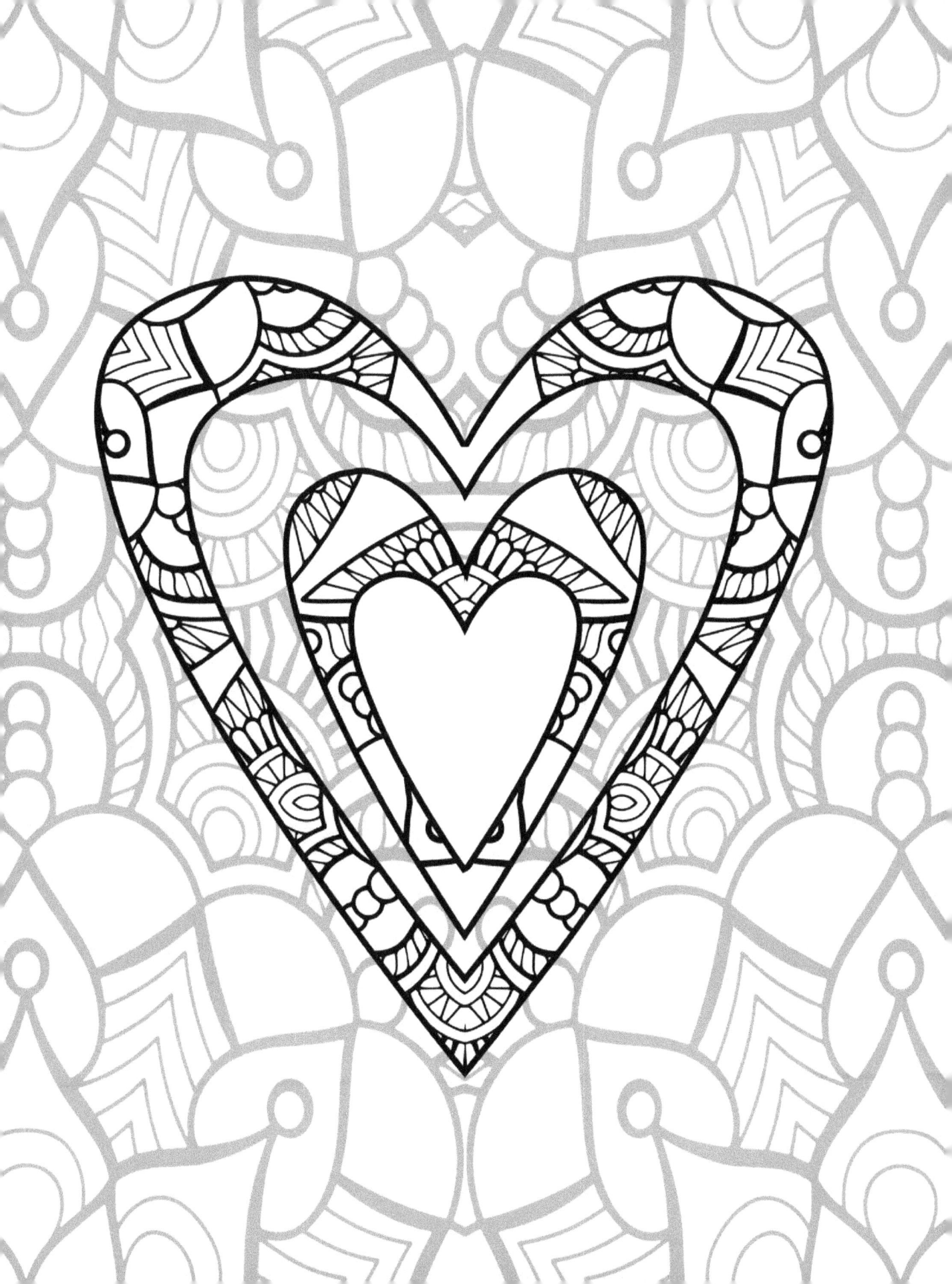

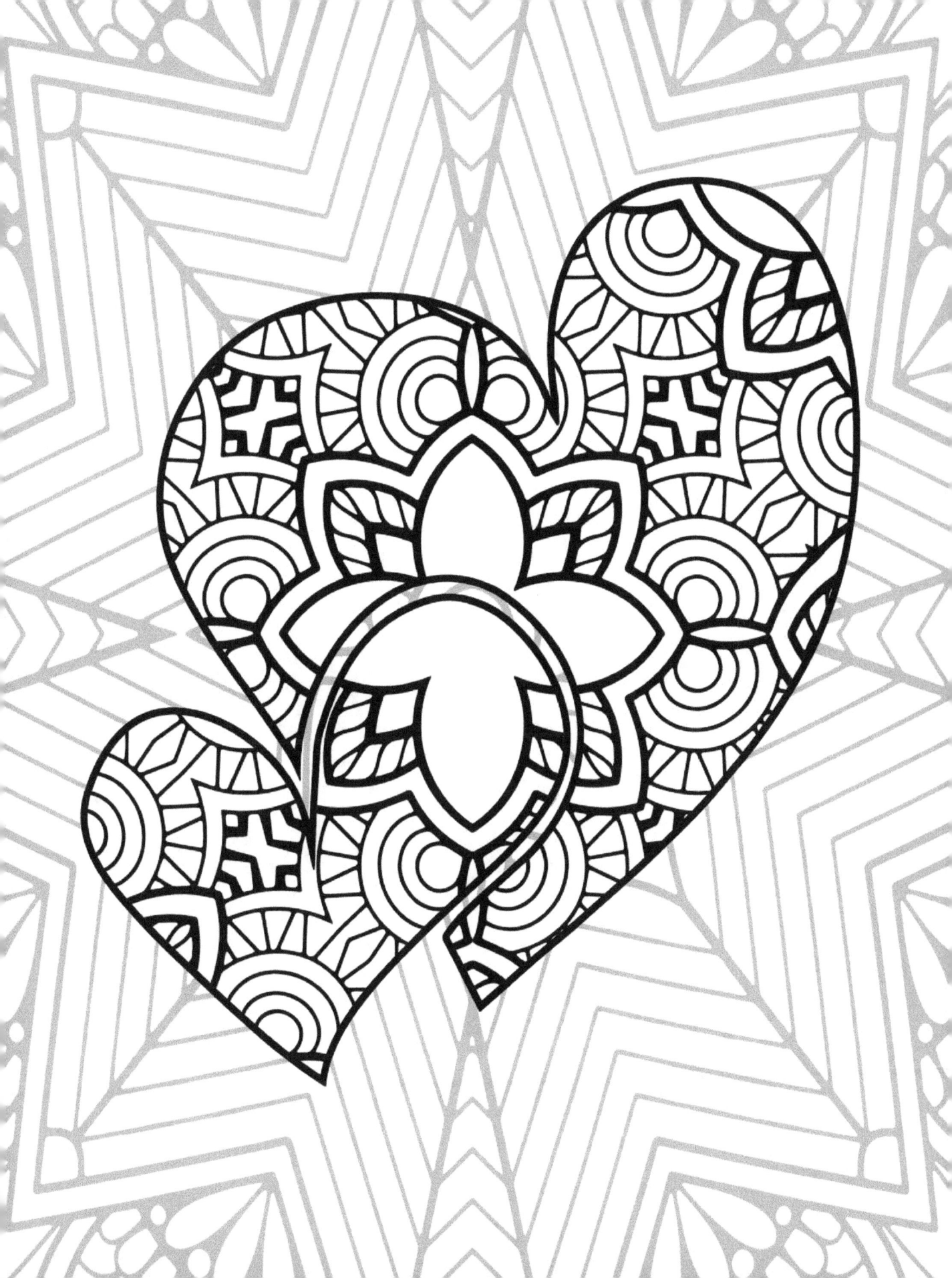

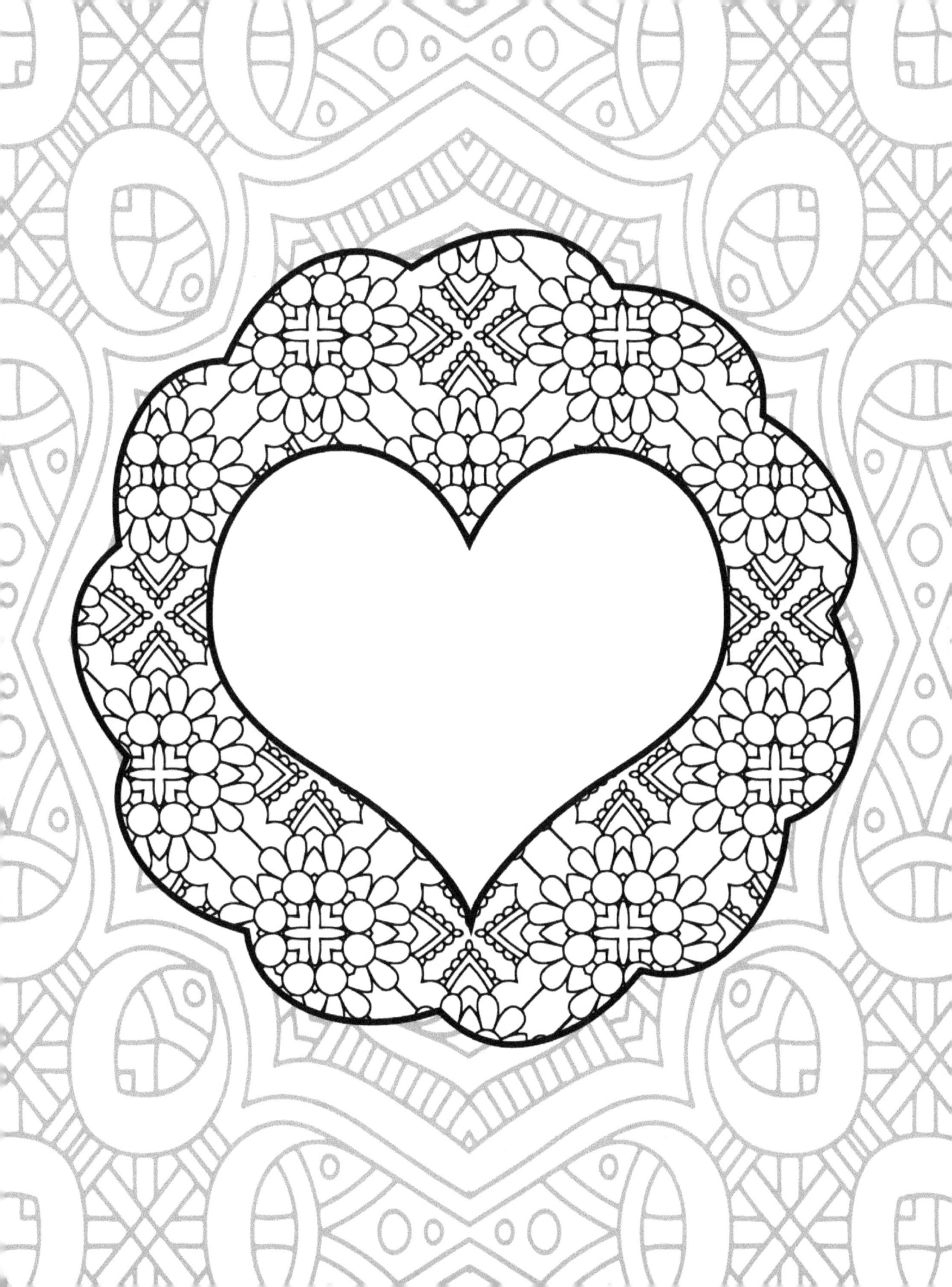

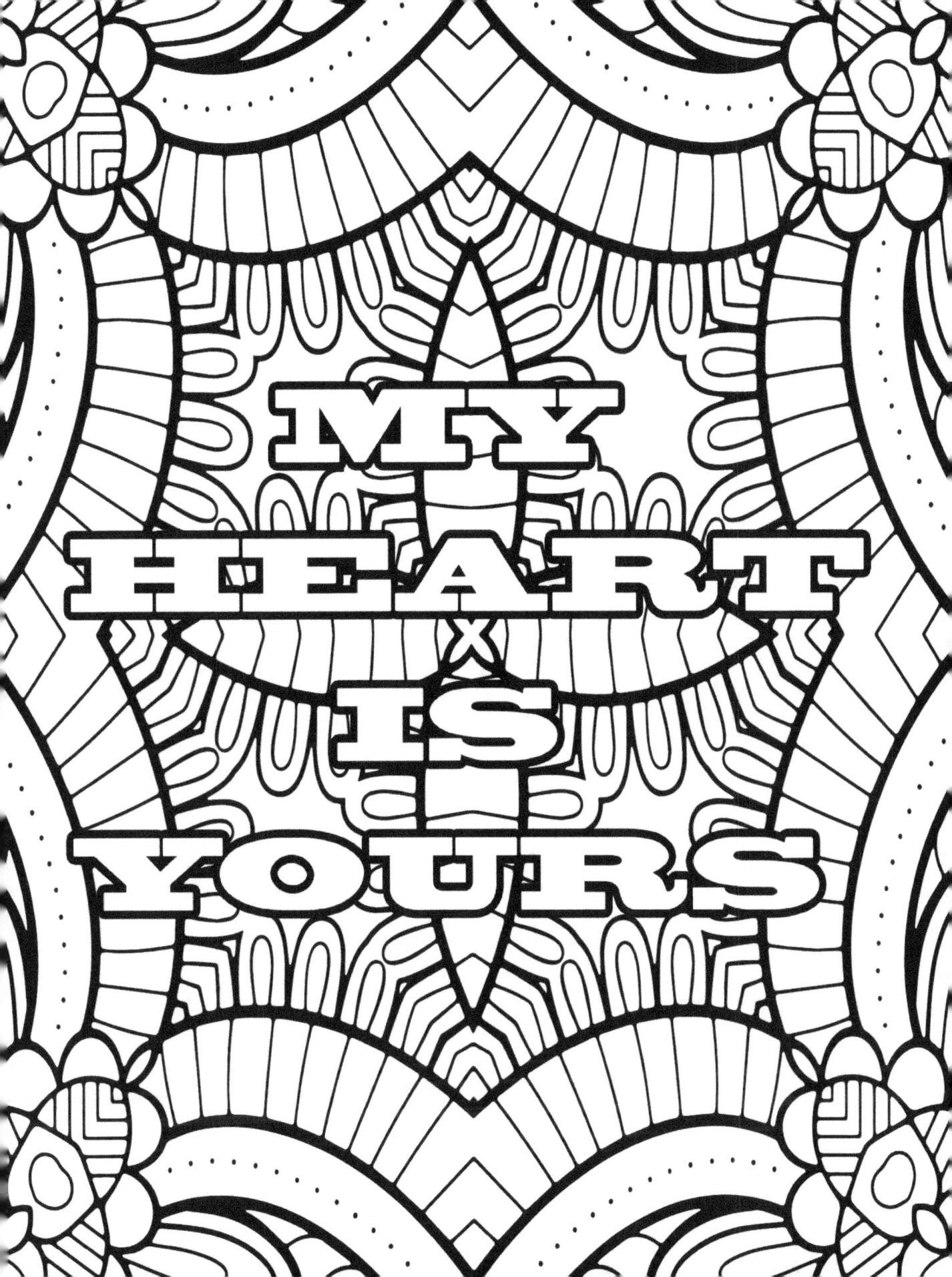

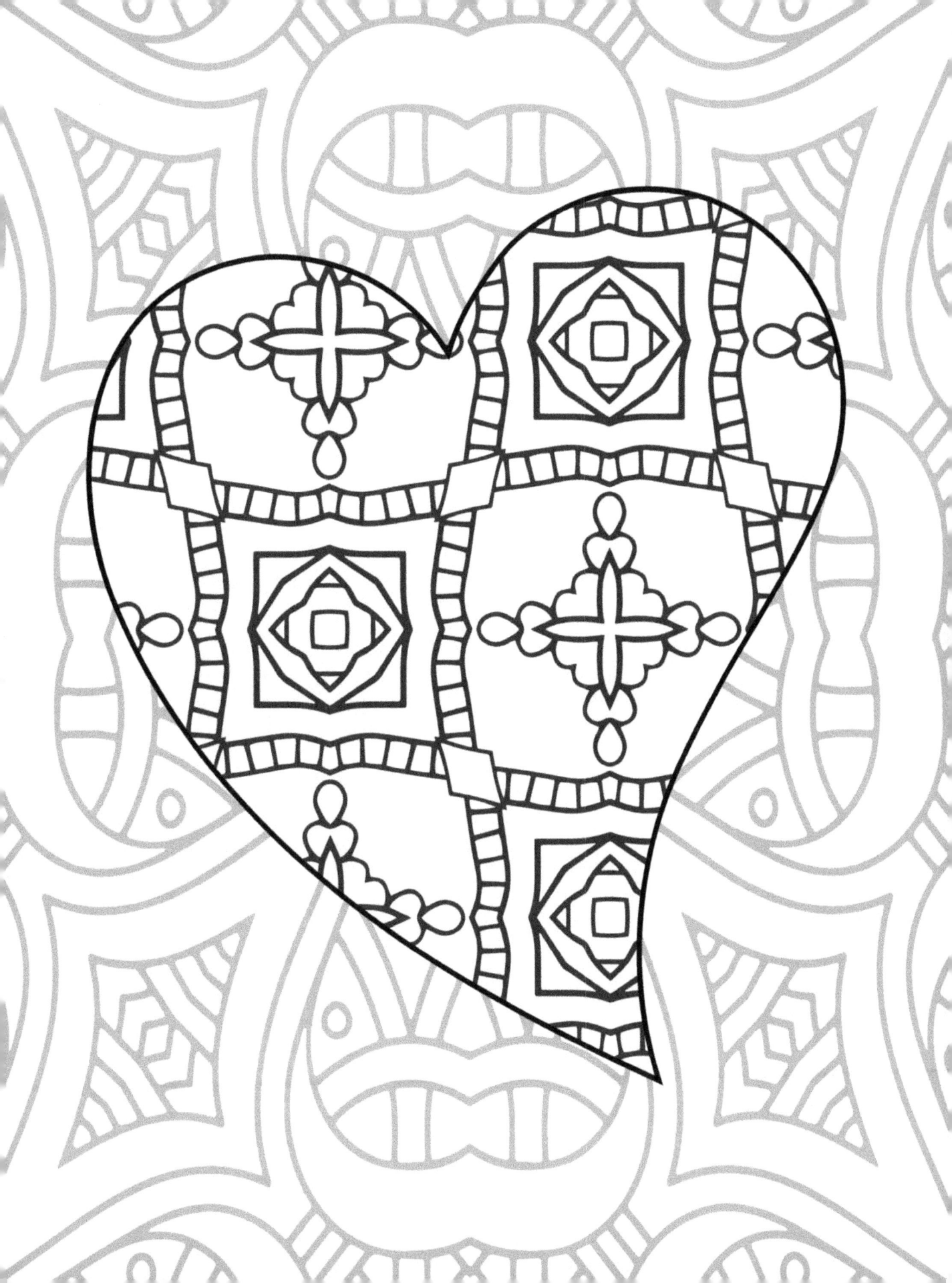

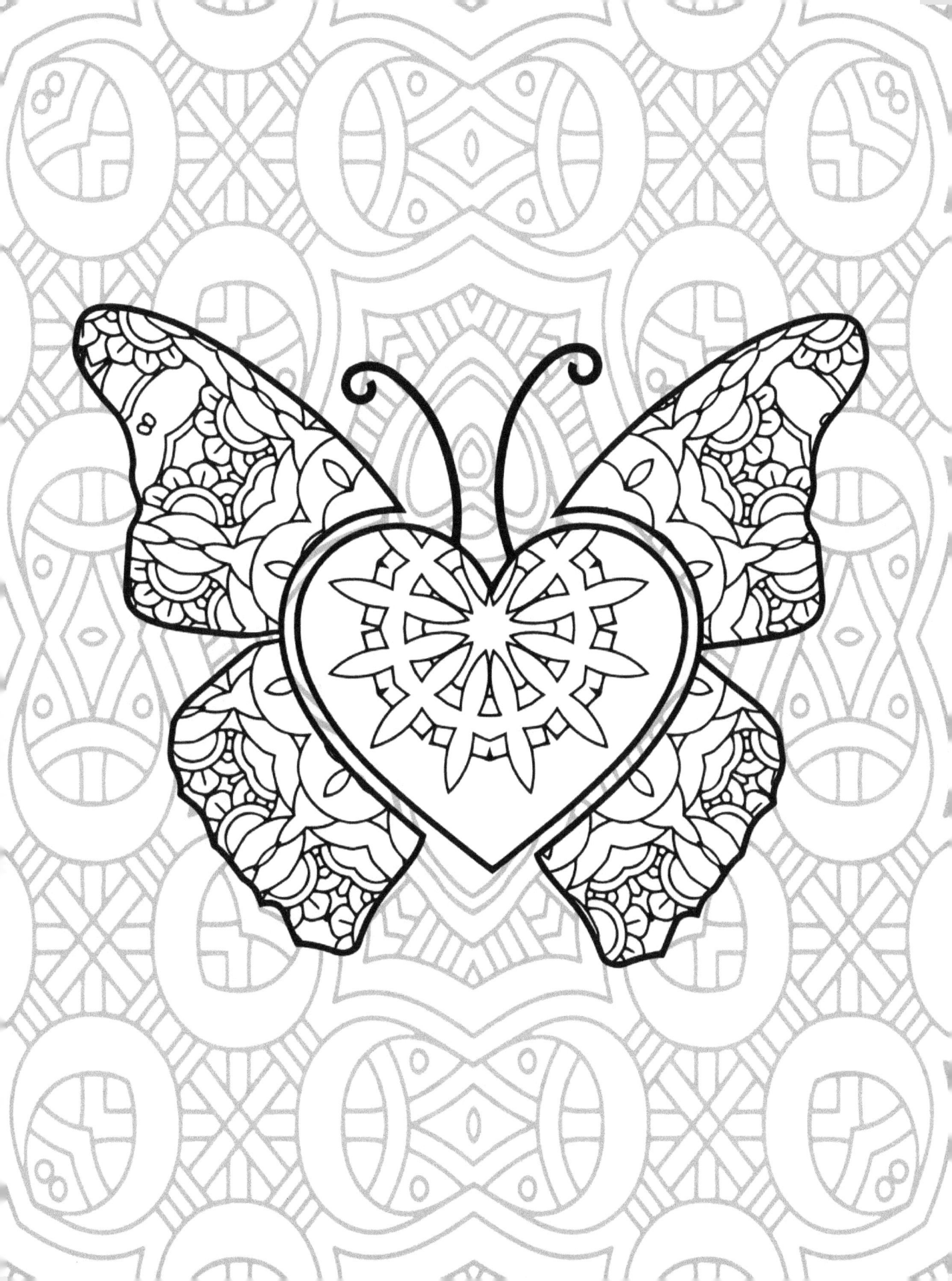

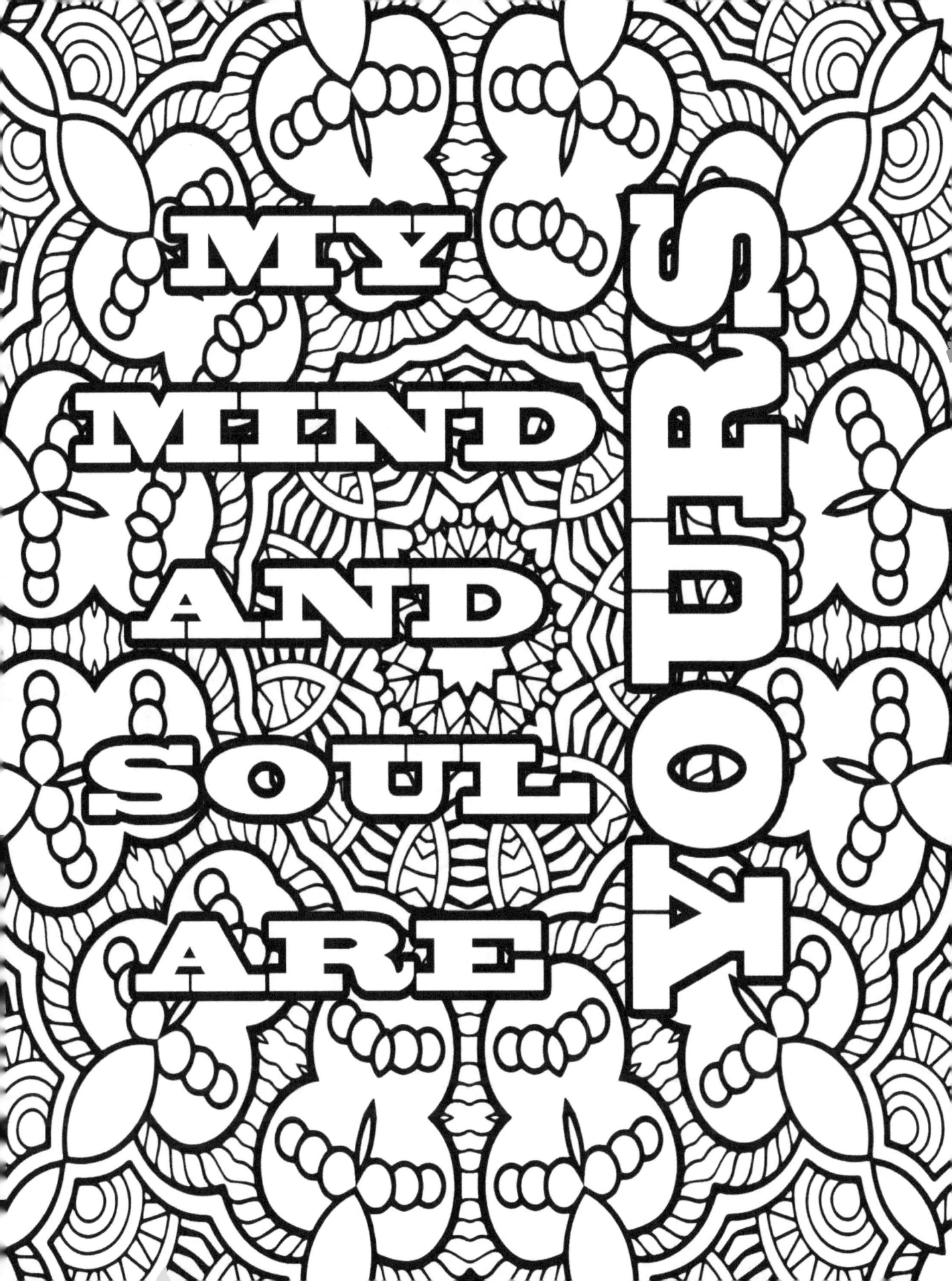

MY MIND AND SOUL ARE SUPER STRONG

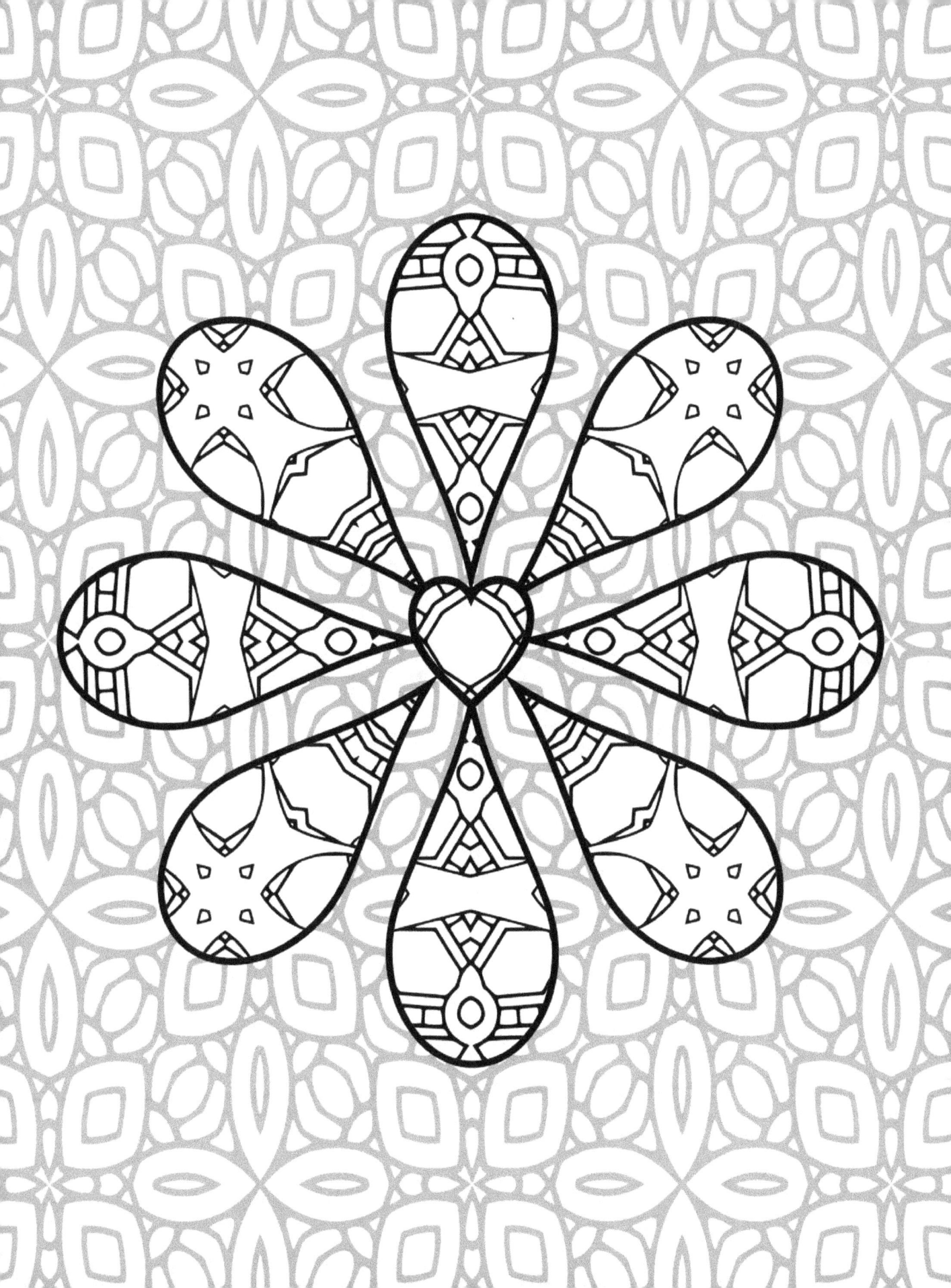

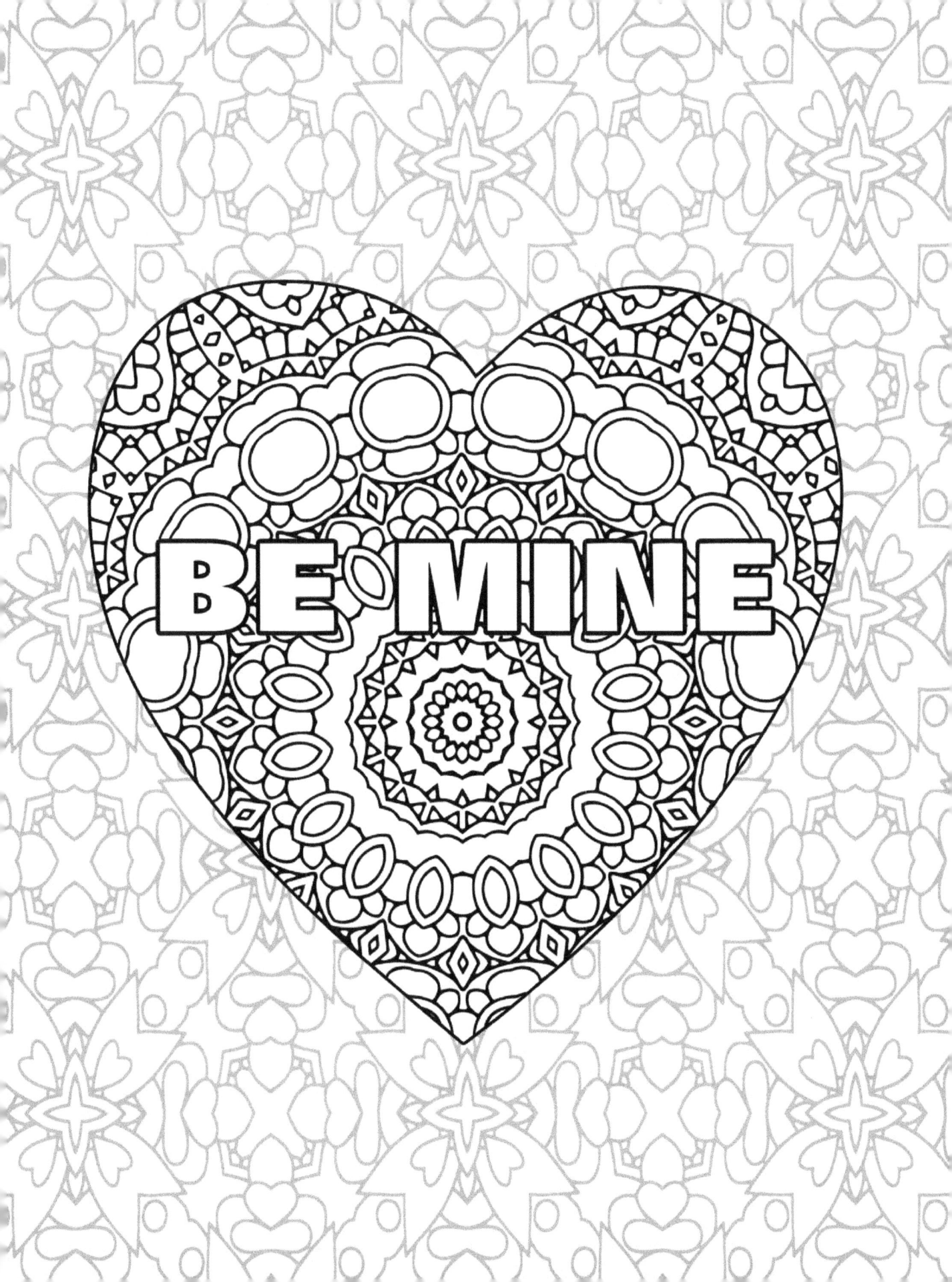

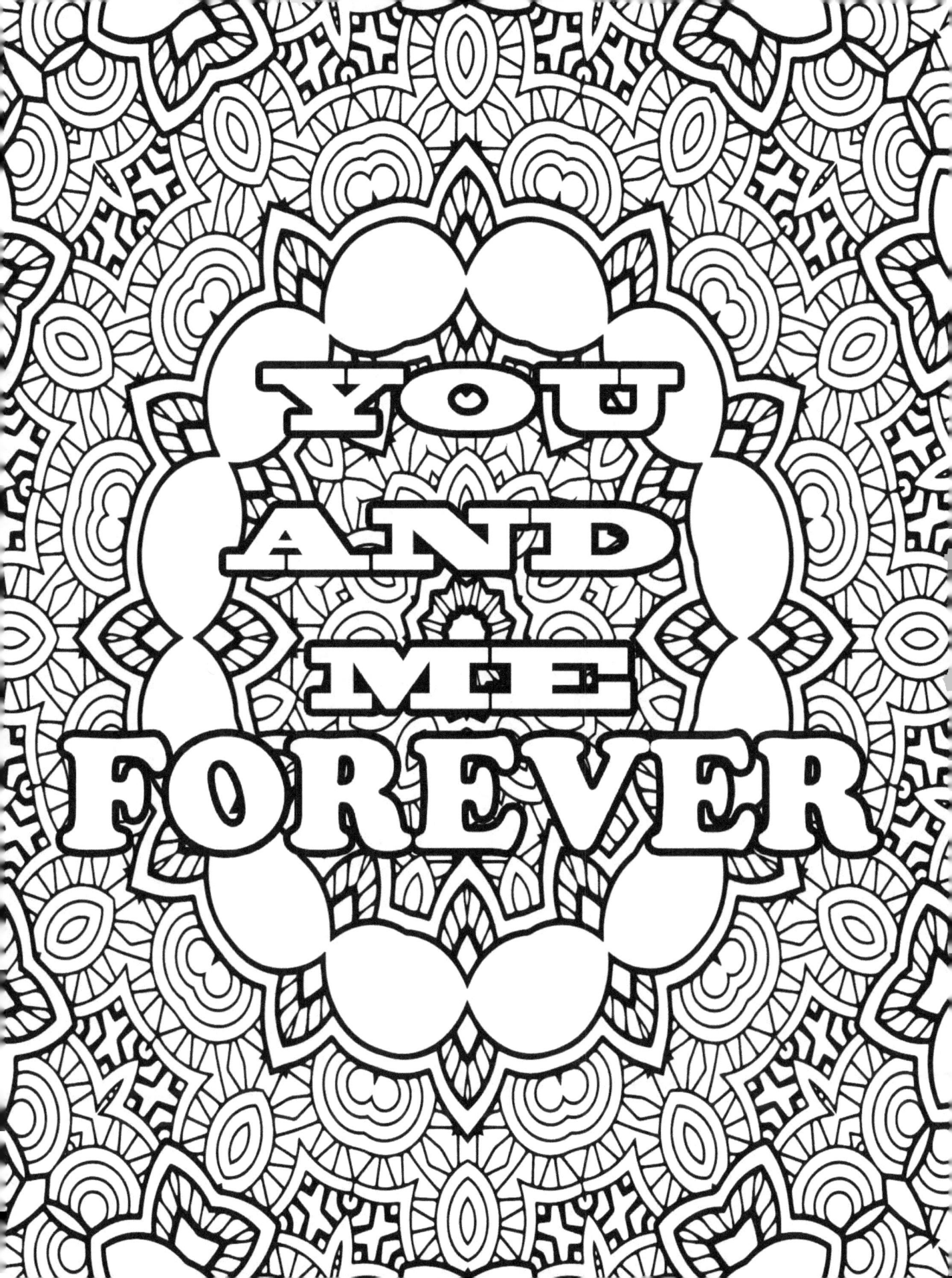

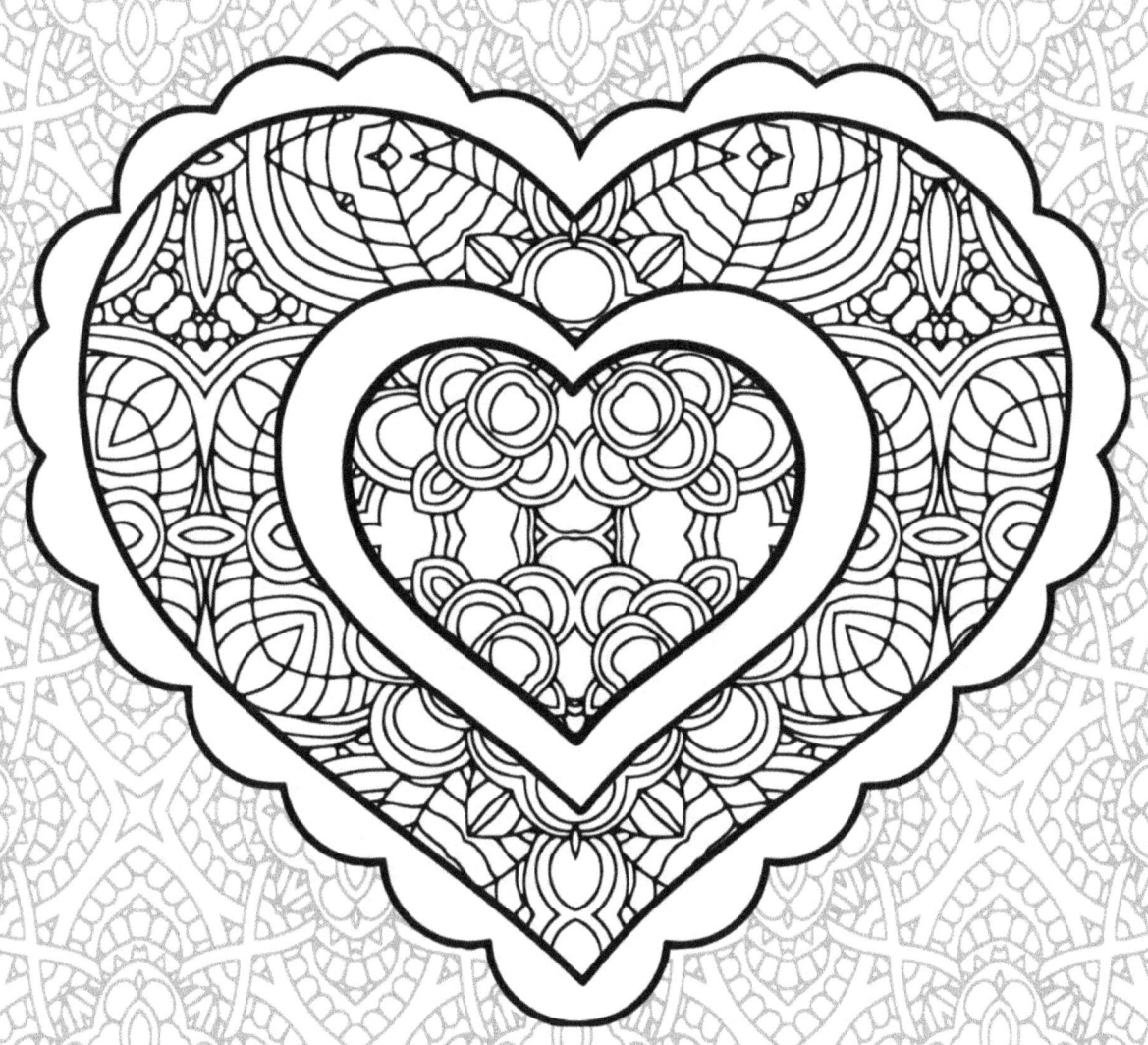

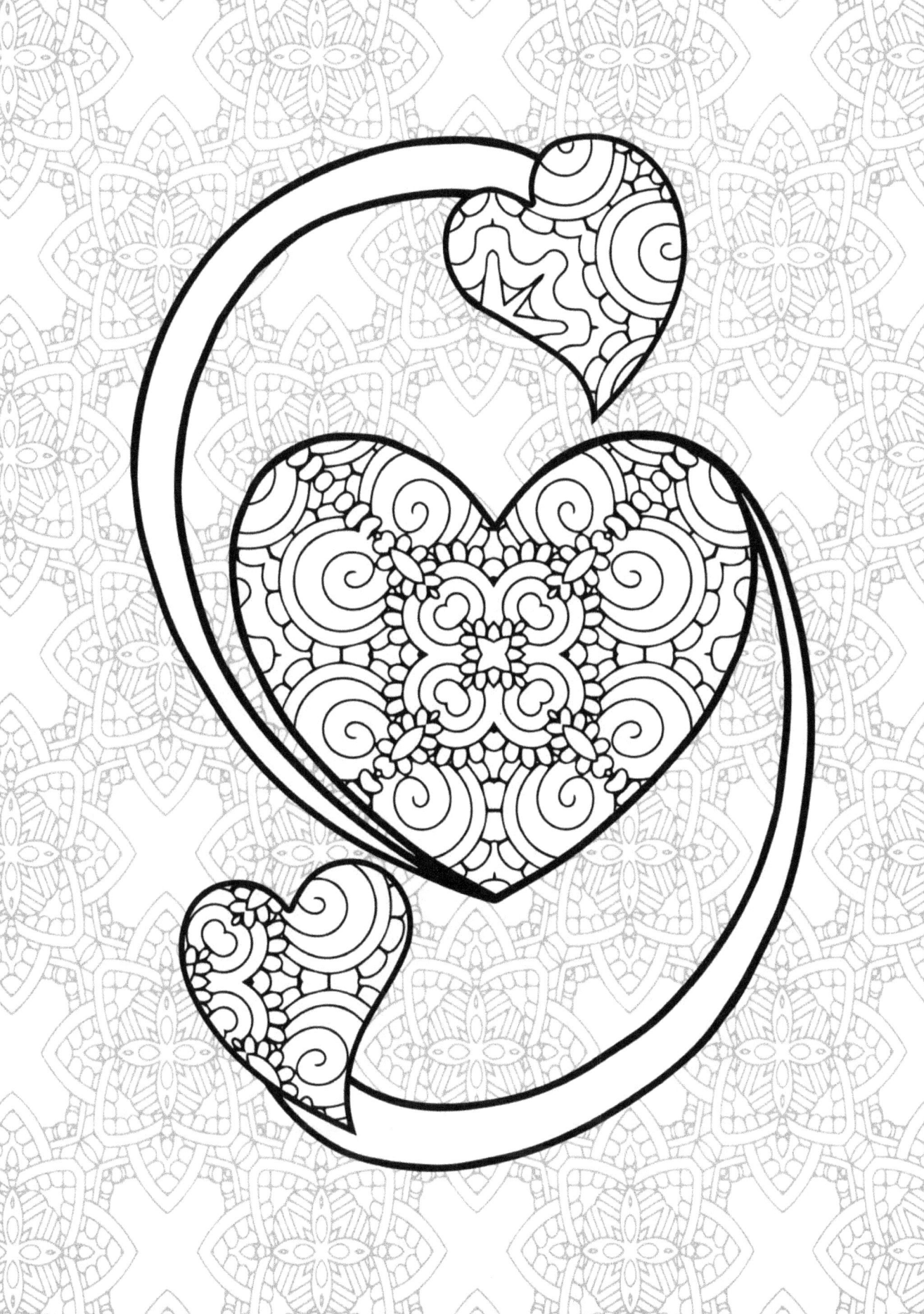

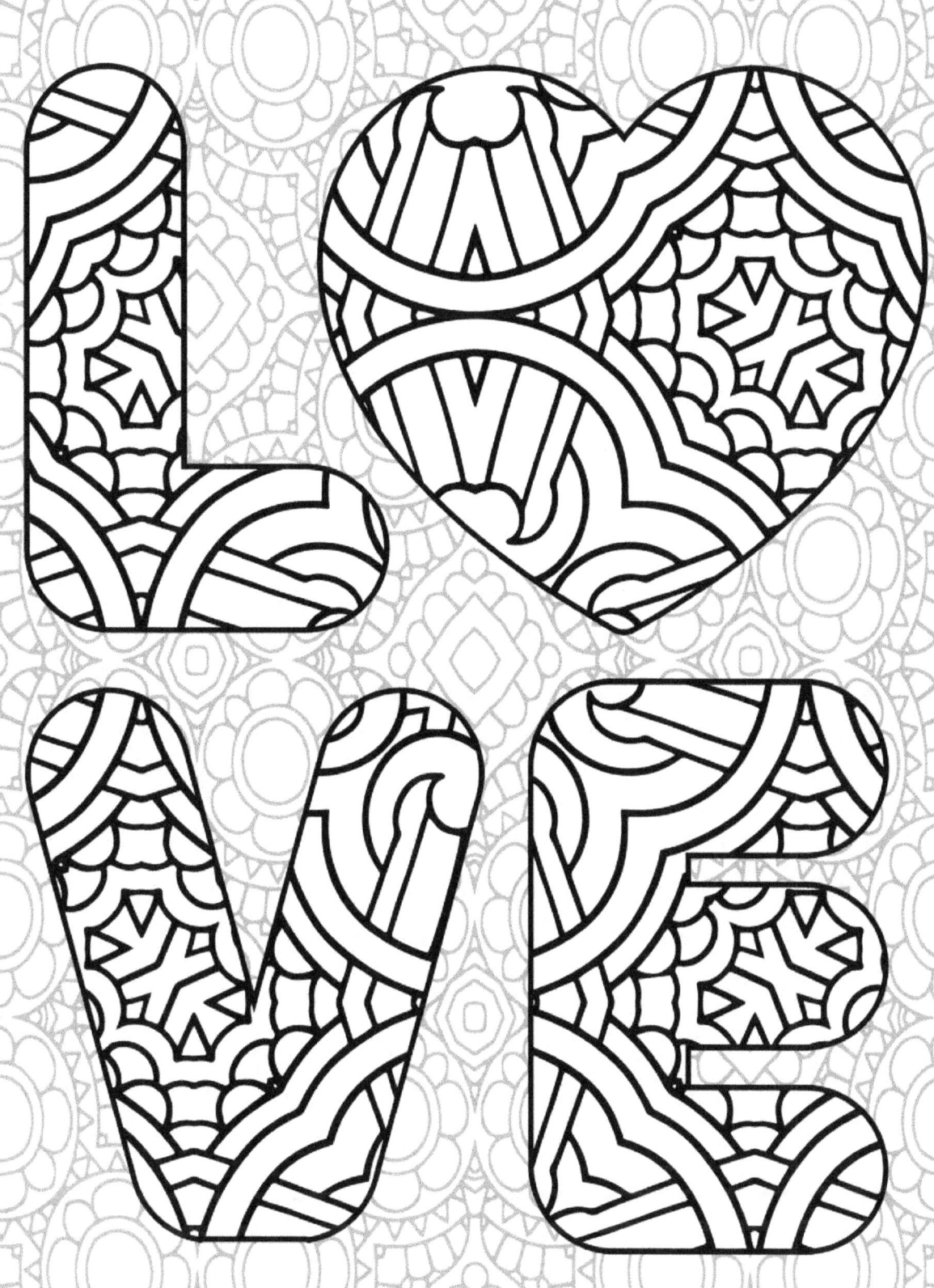

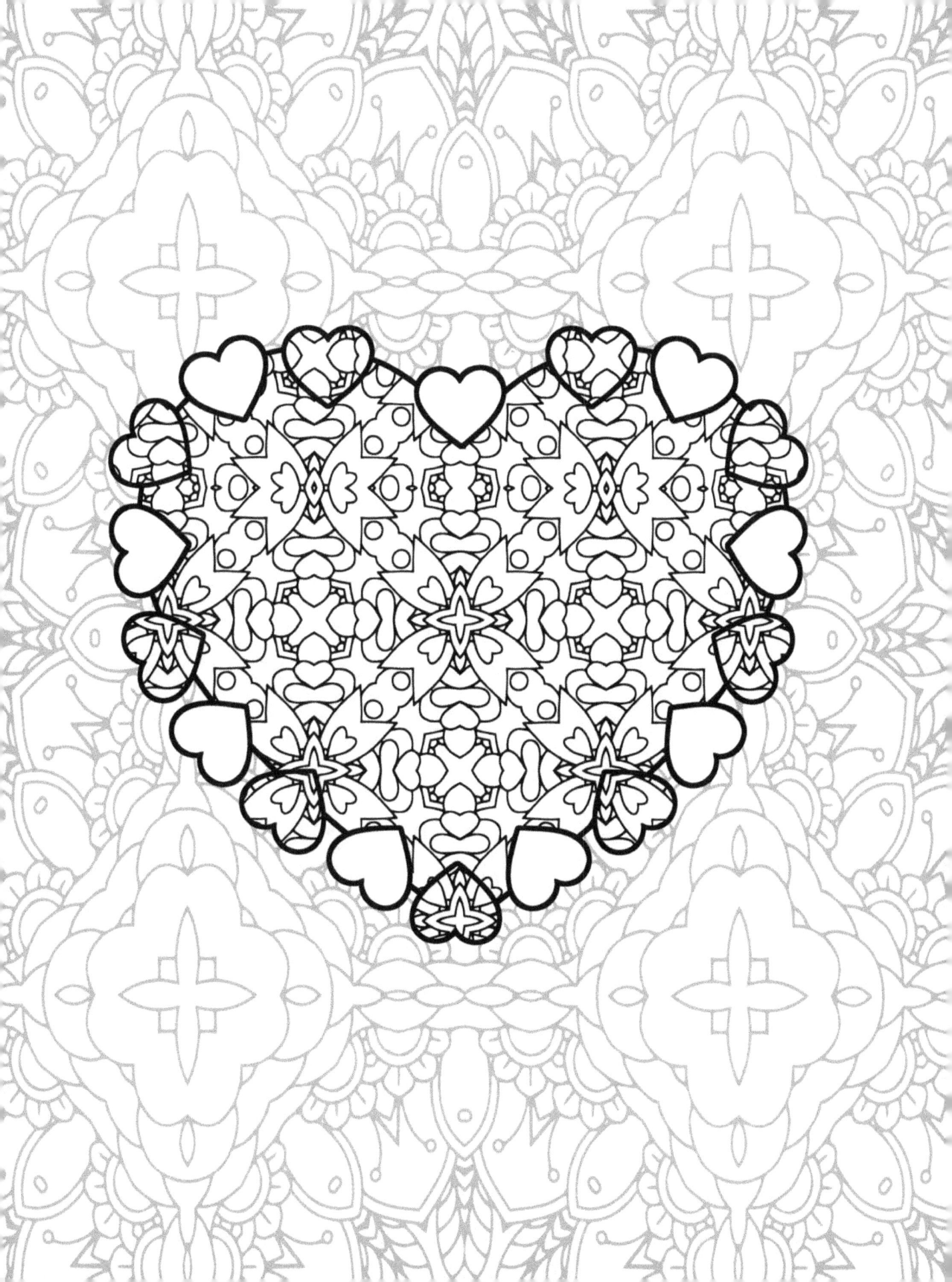

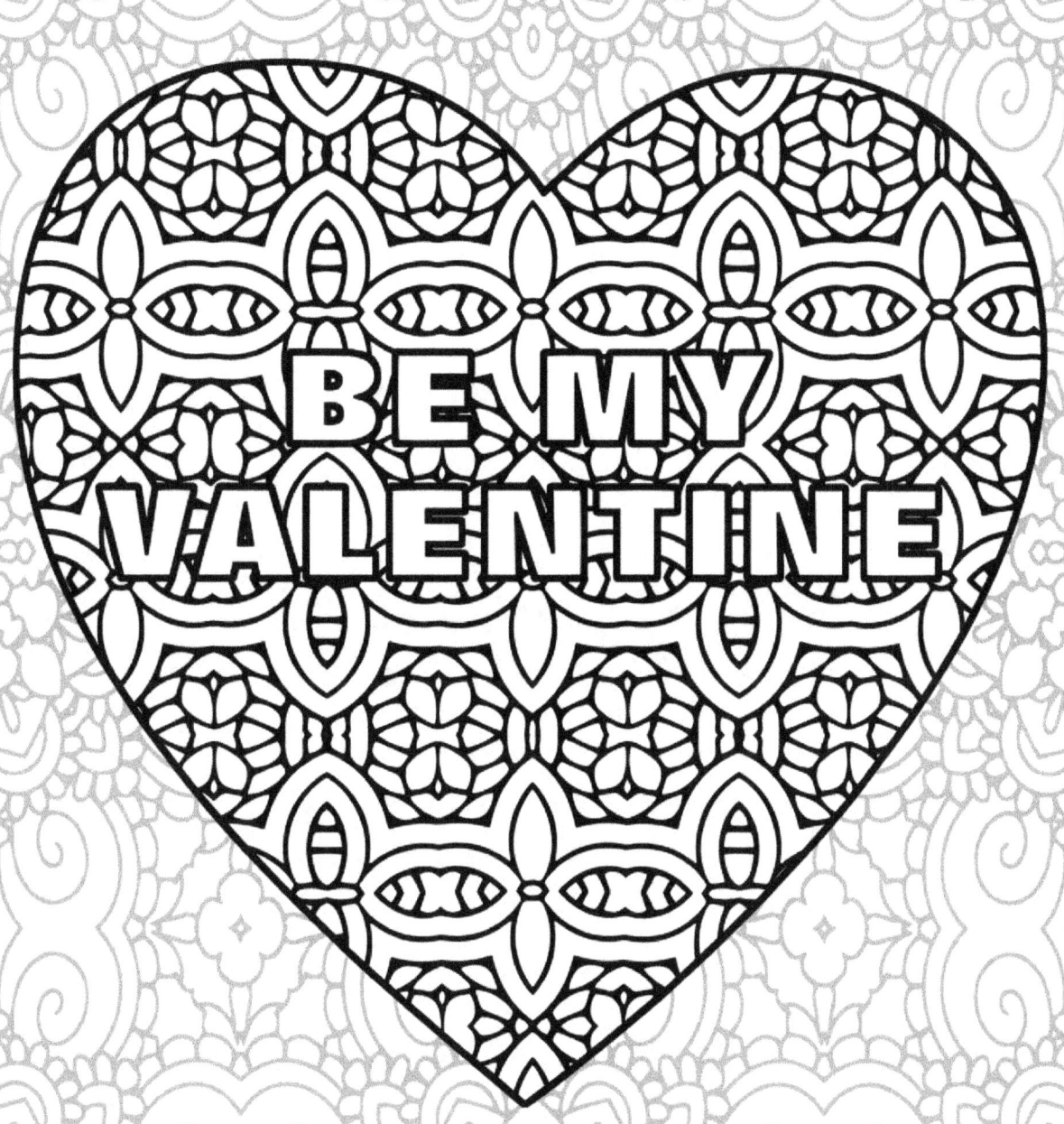

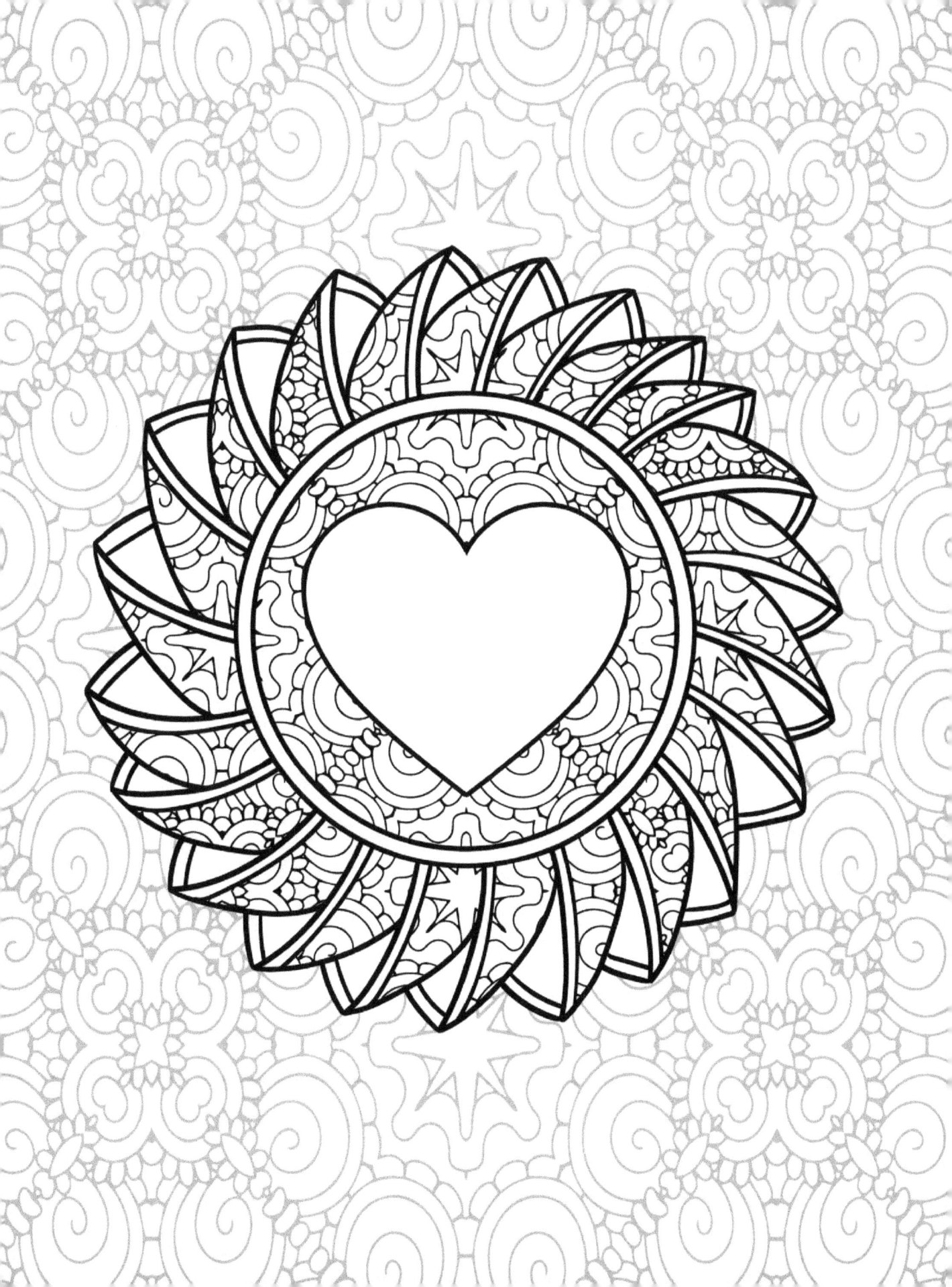

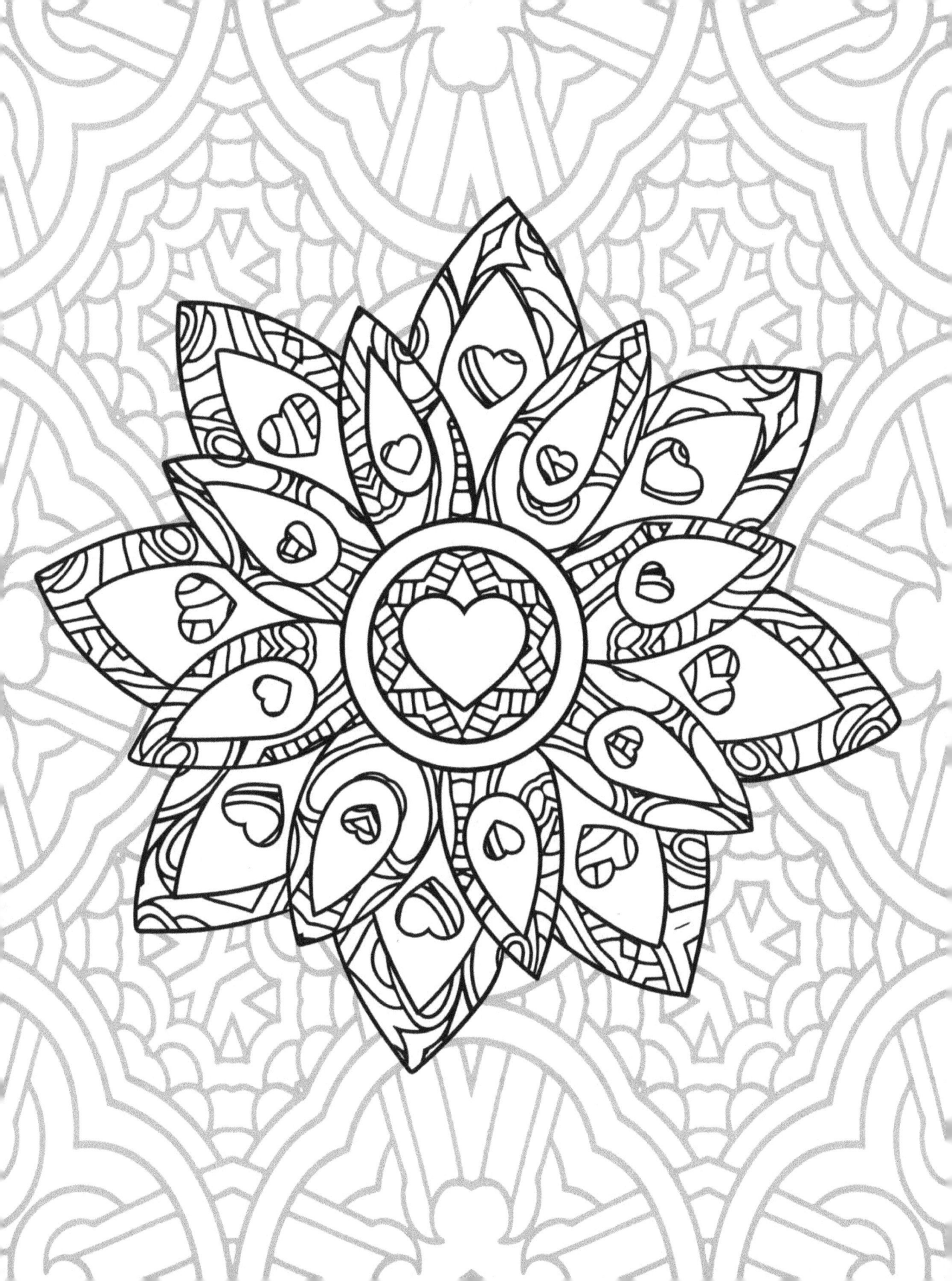

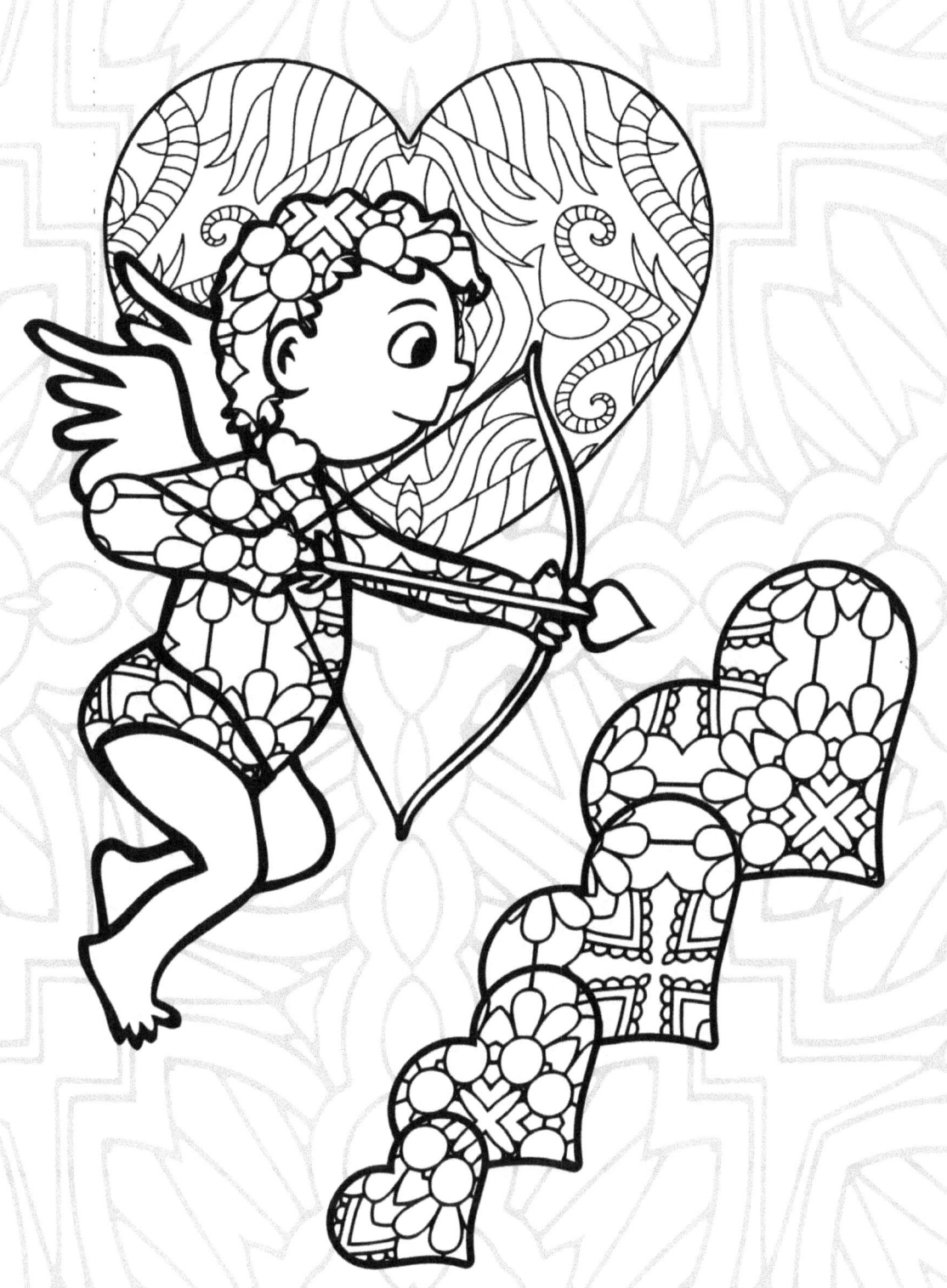

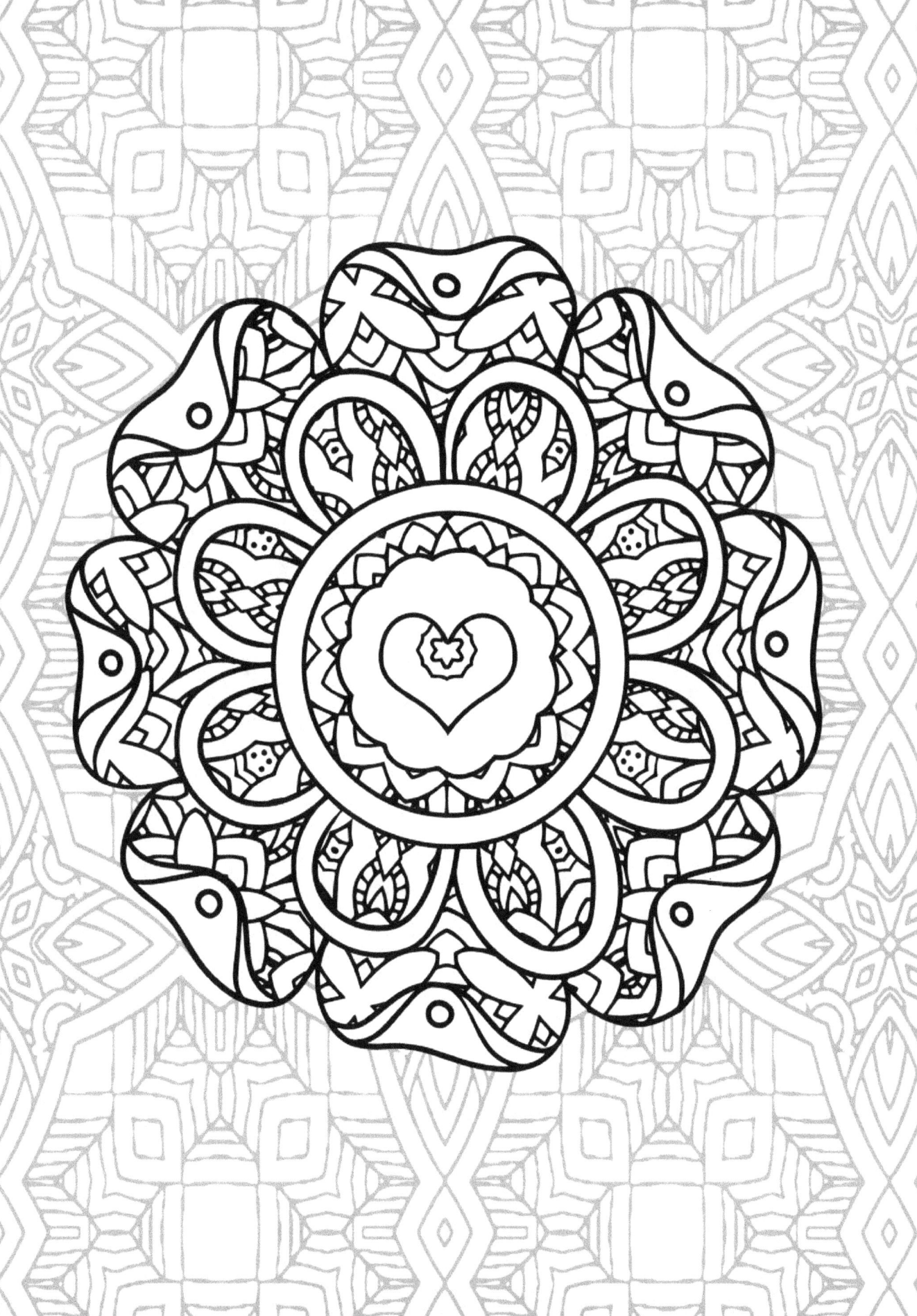

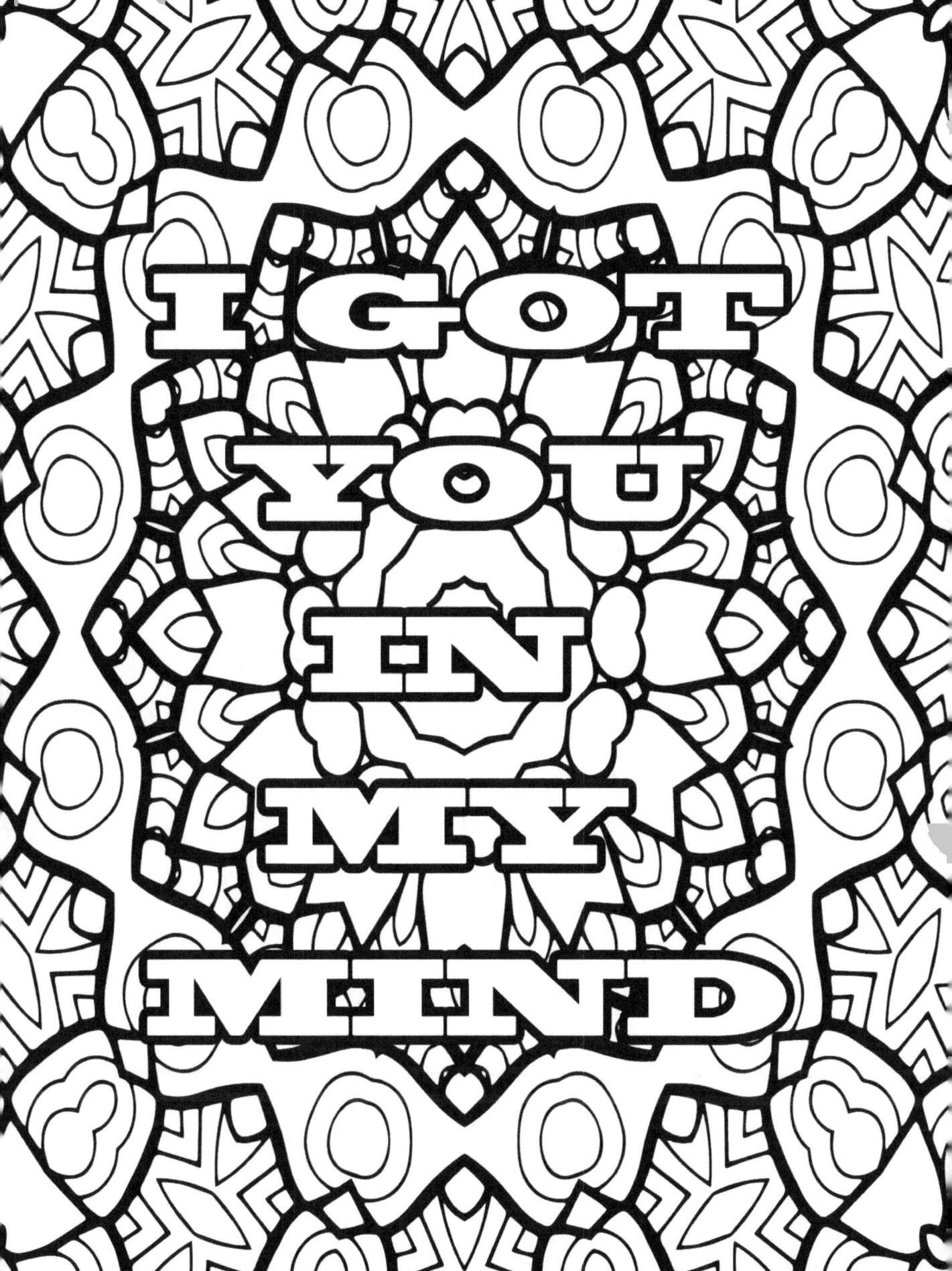

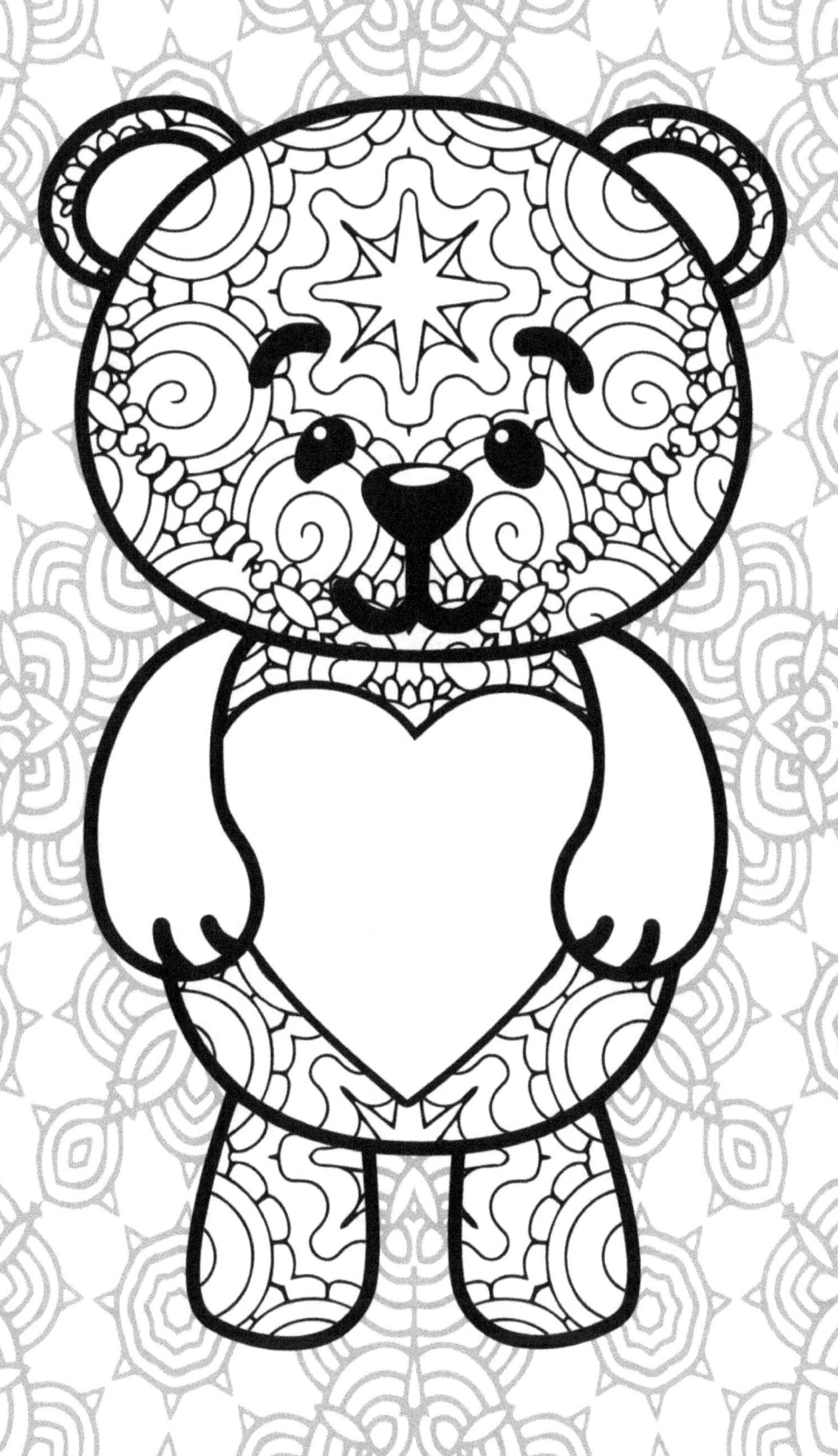

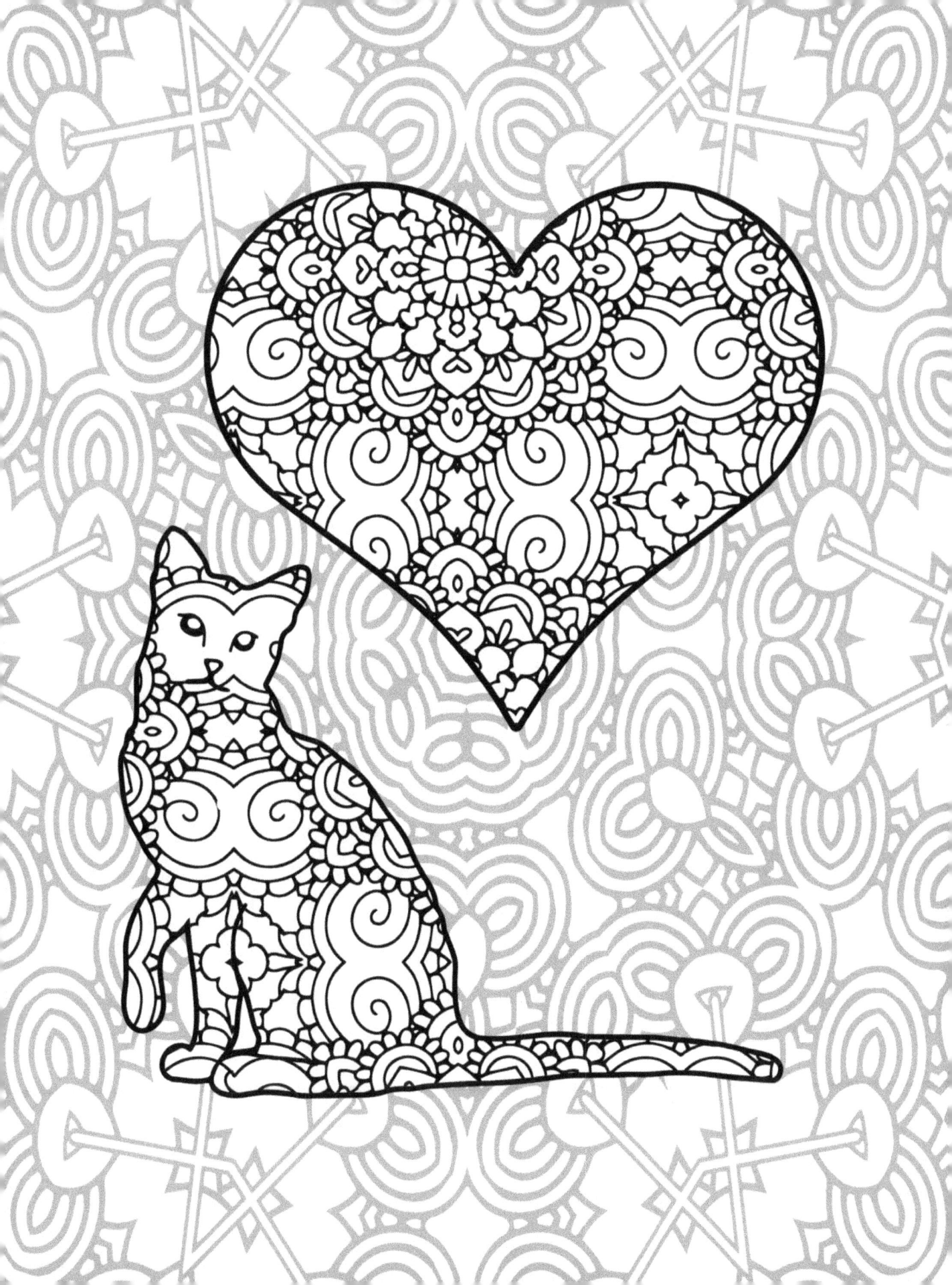

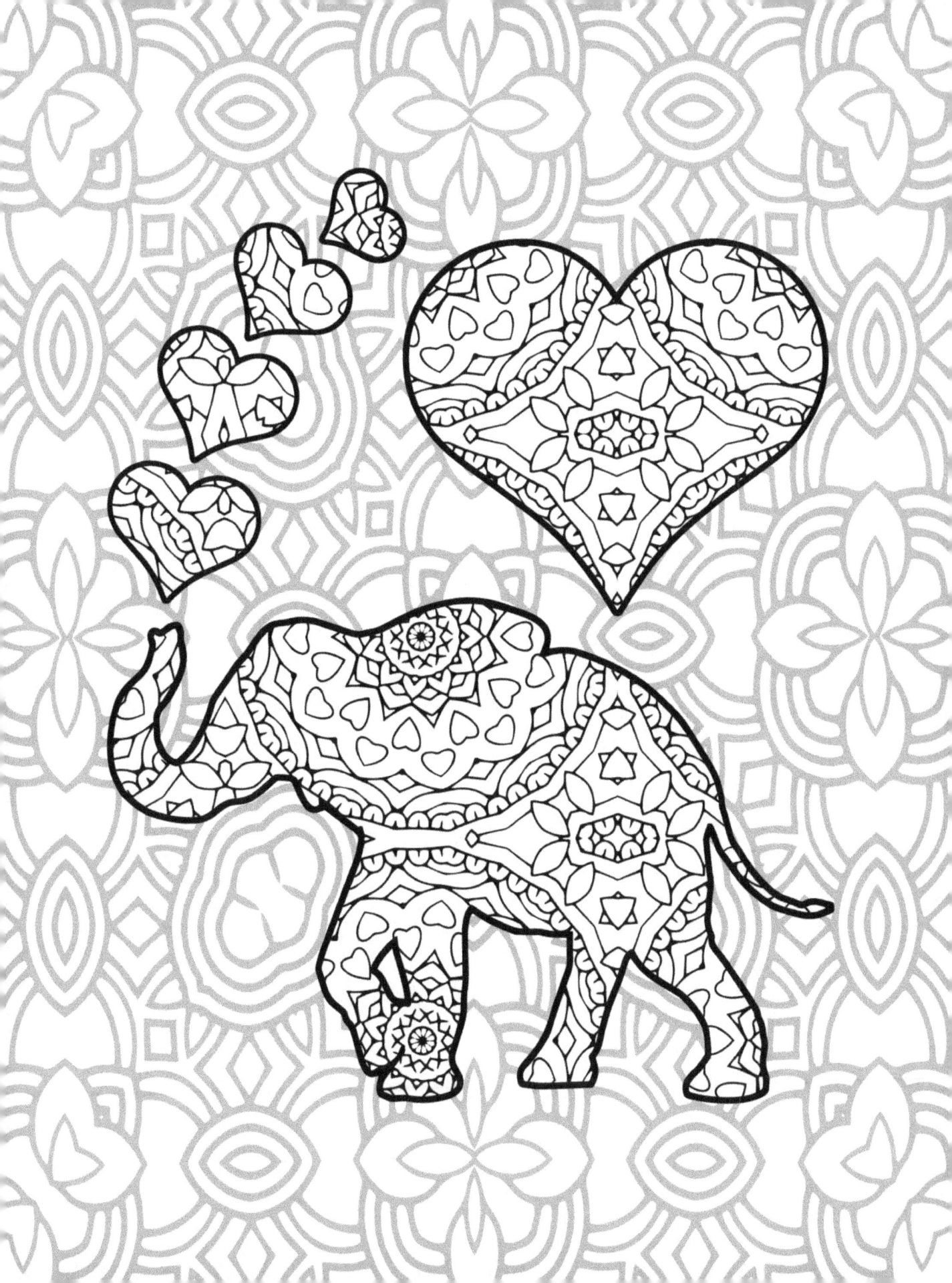

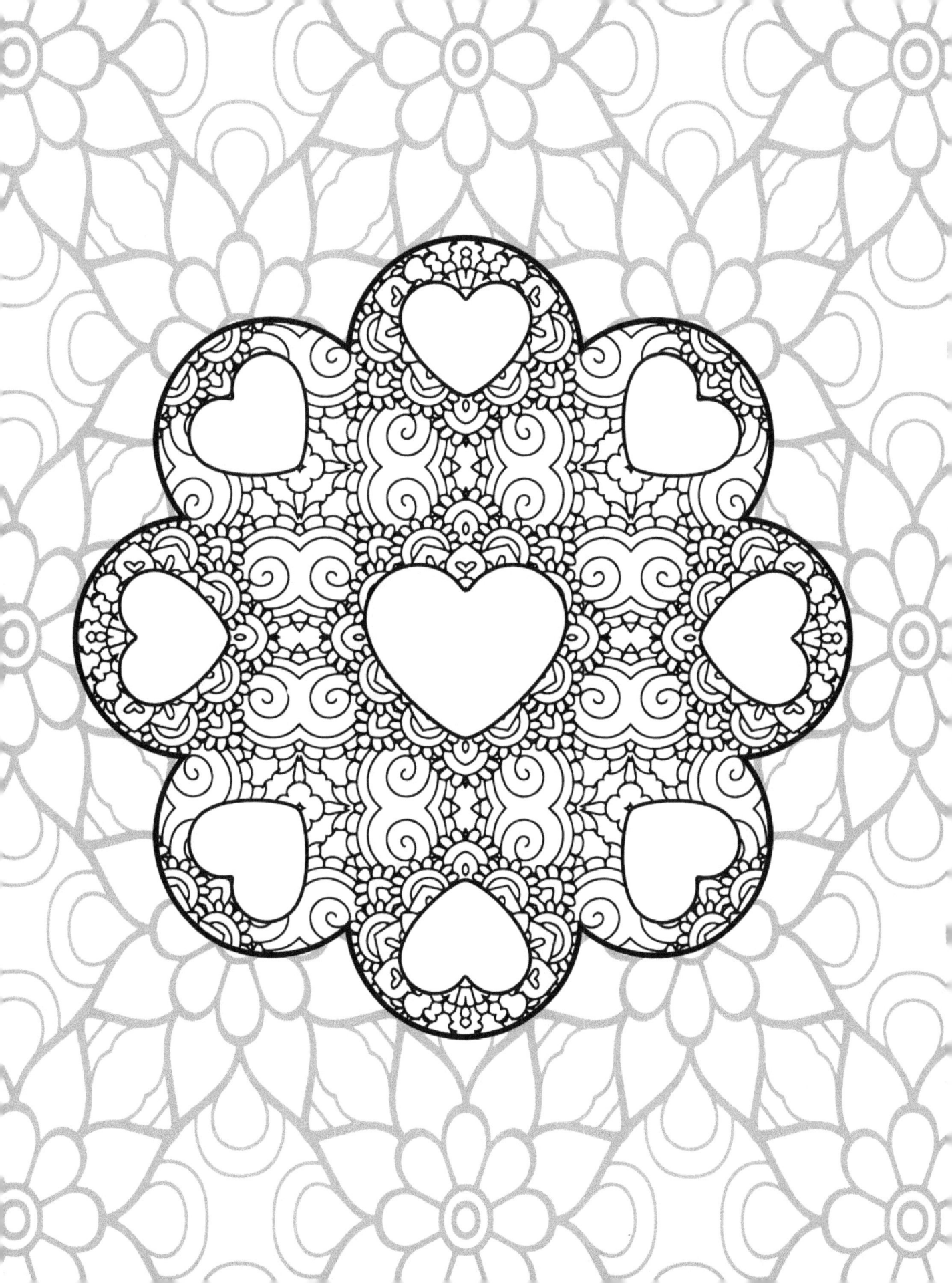

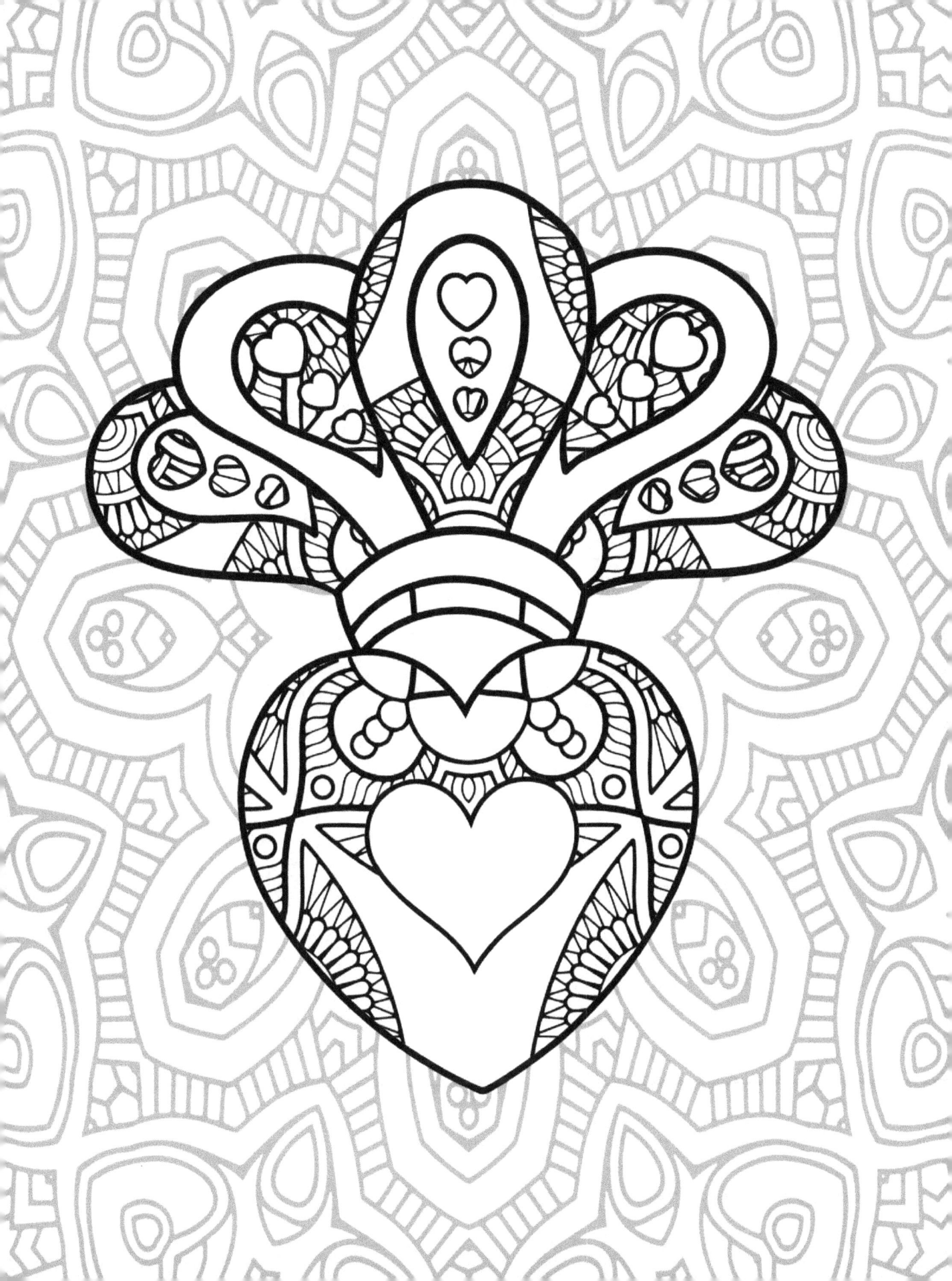

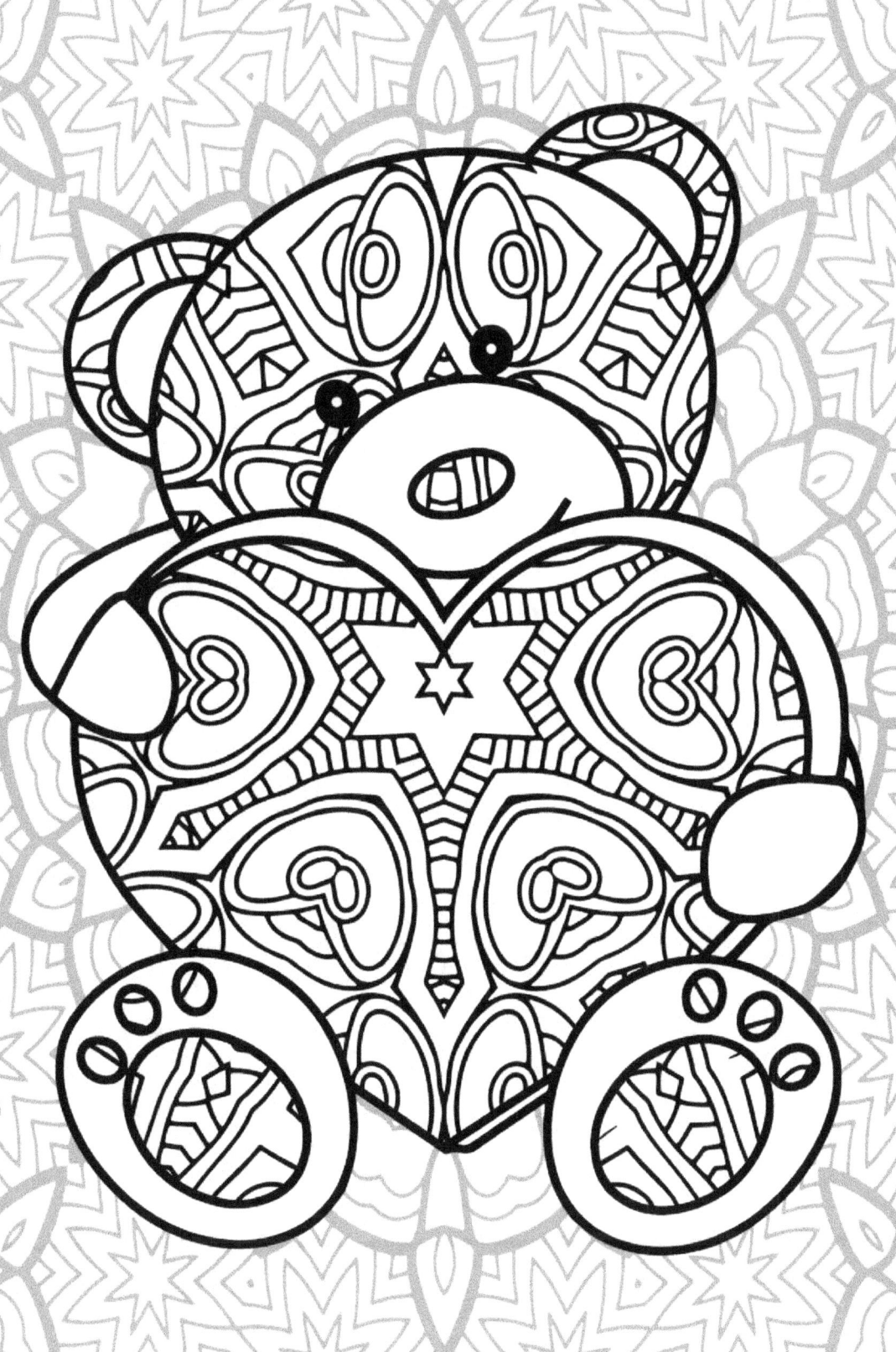

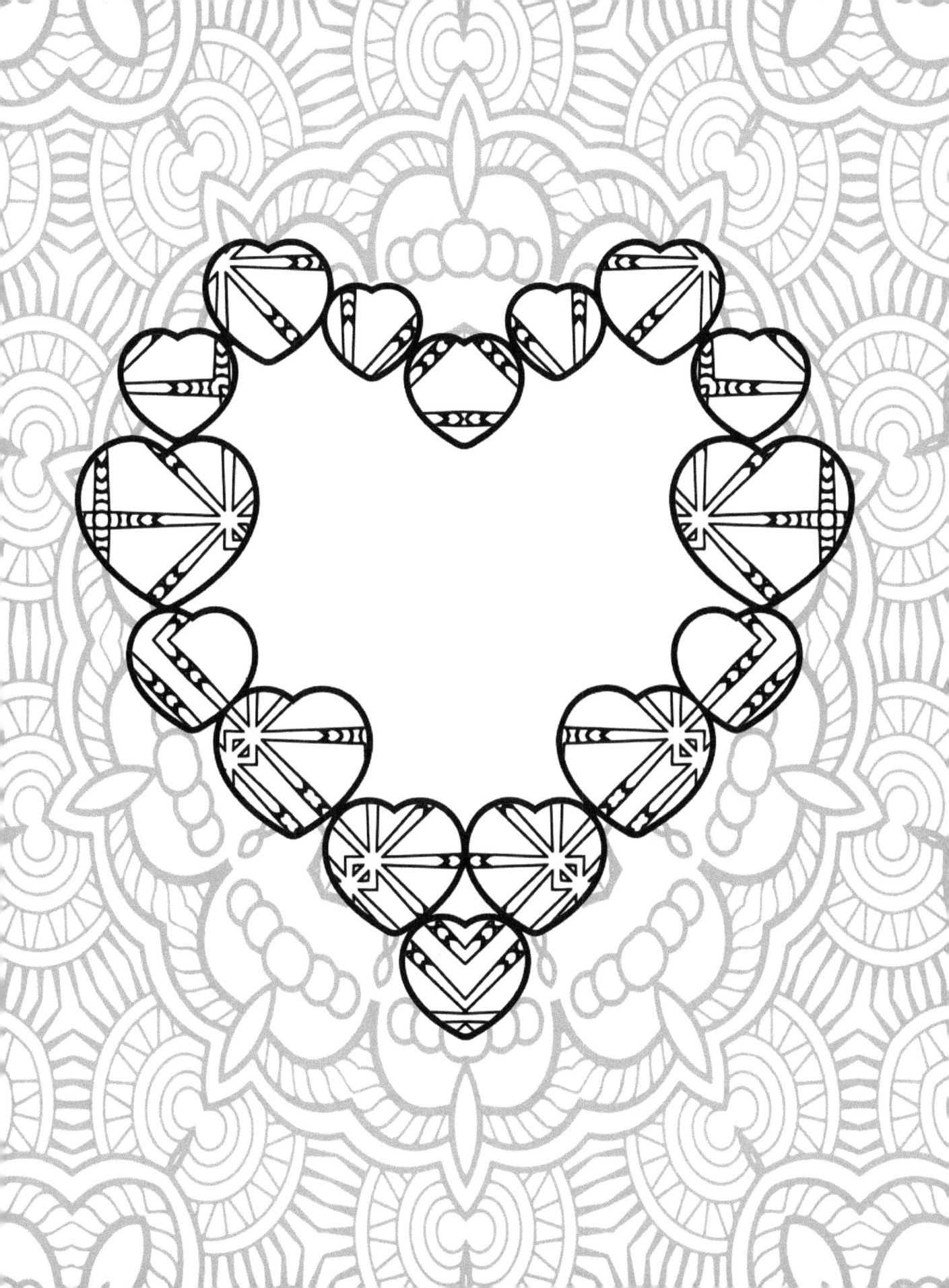

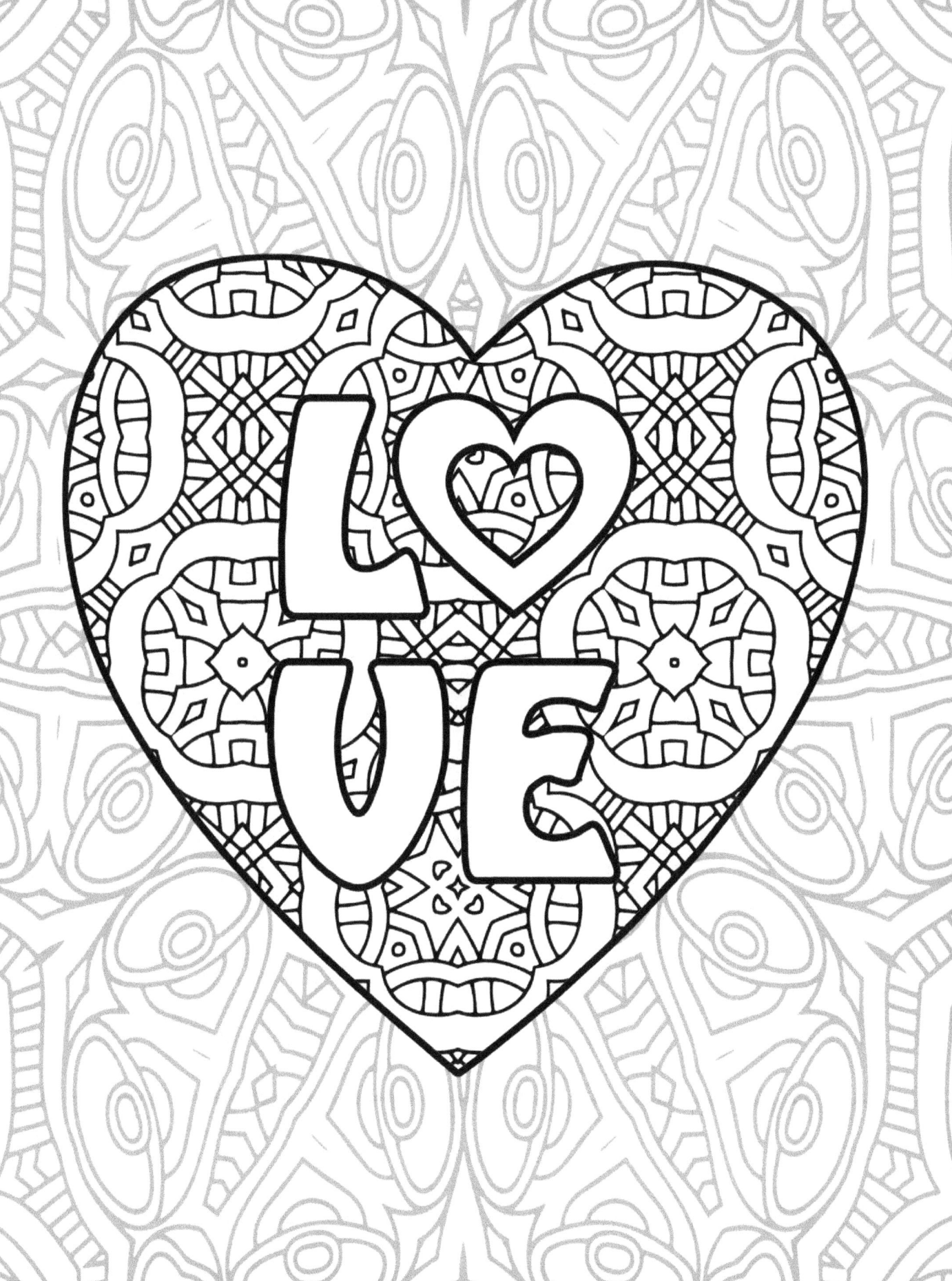

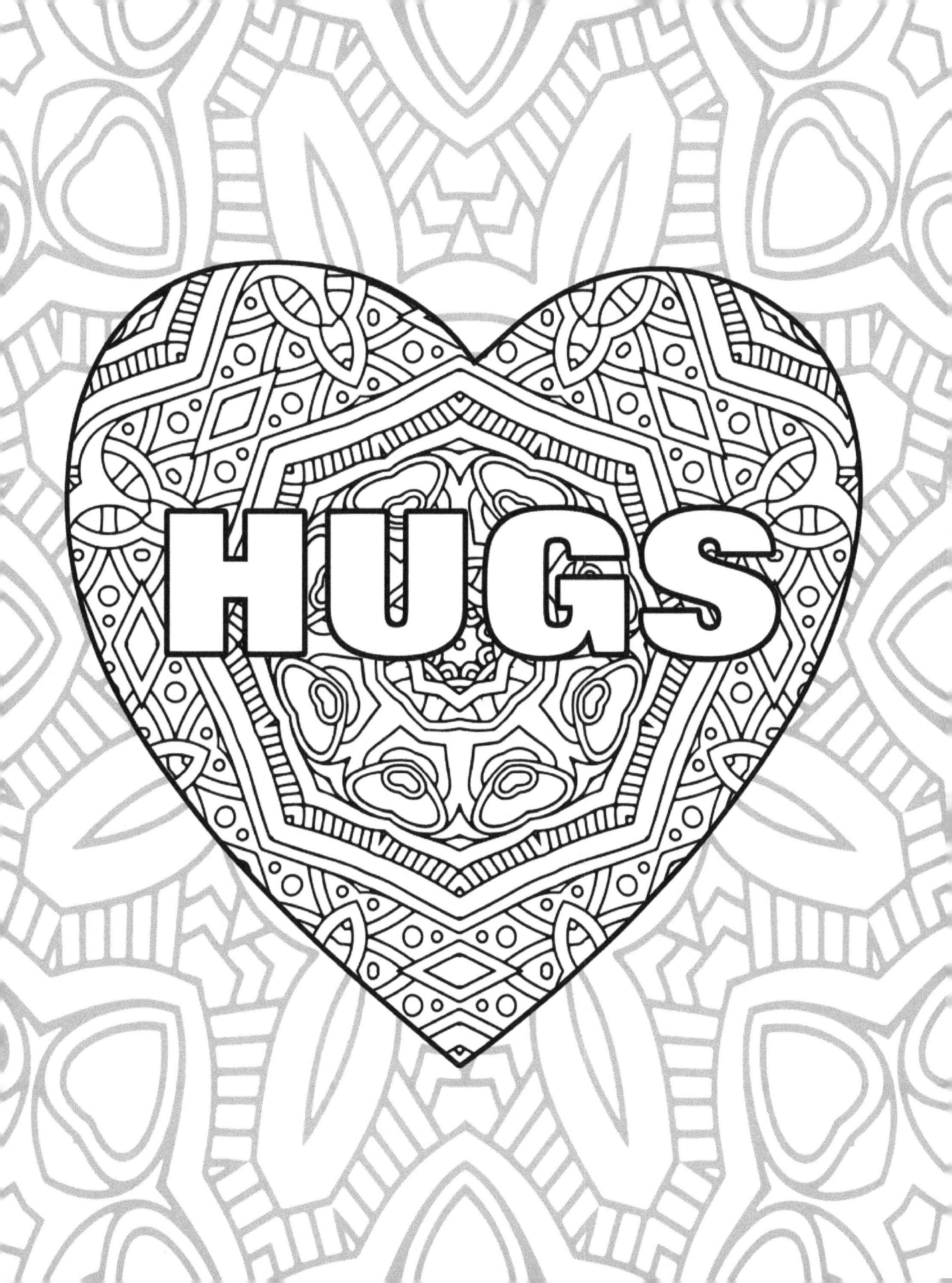

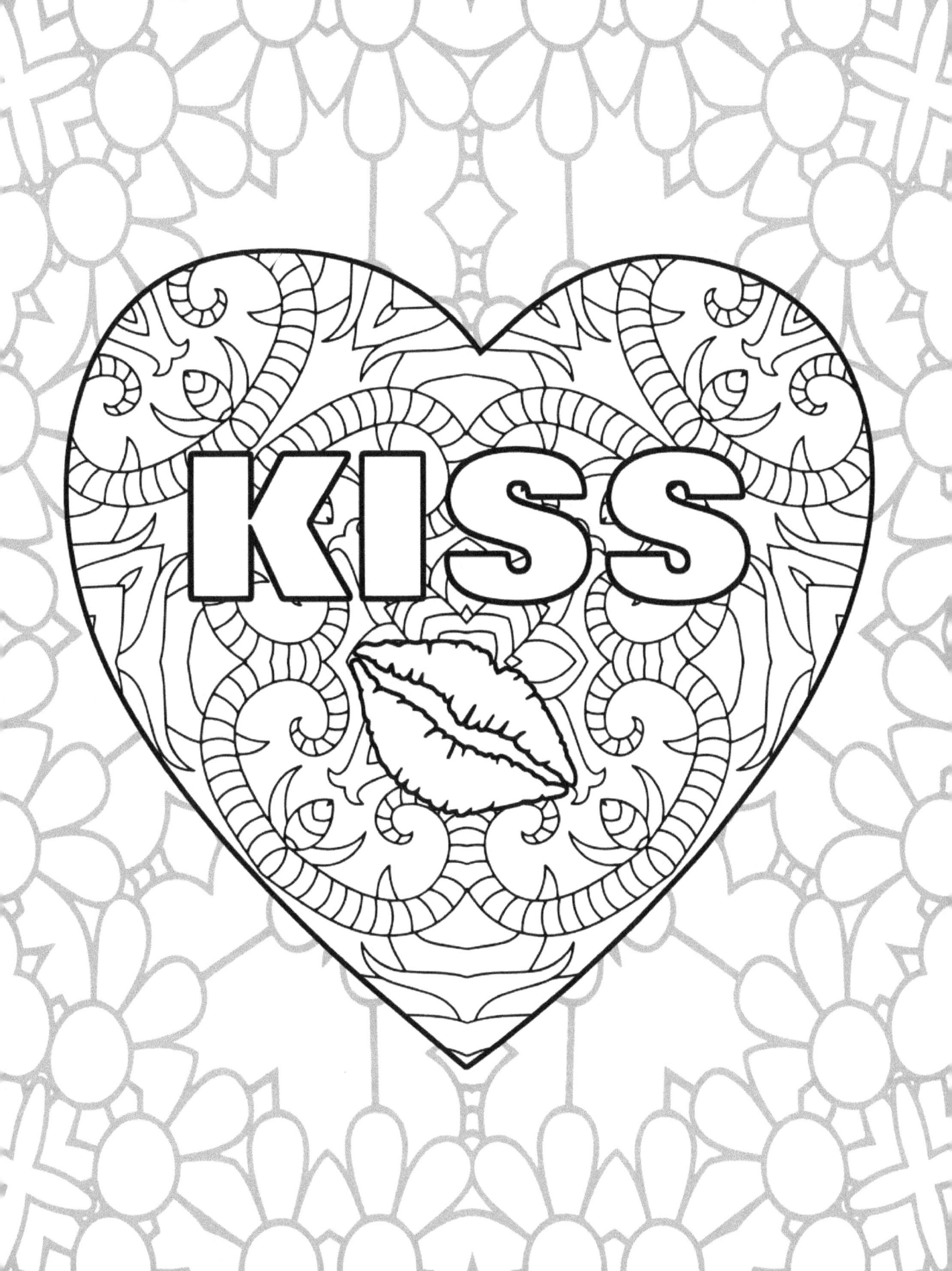

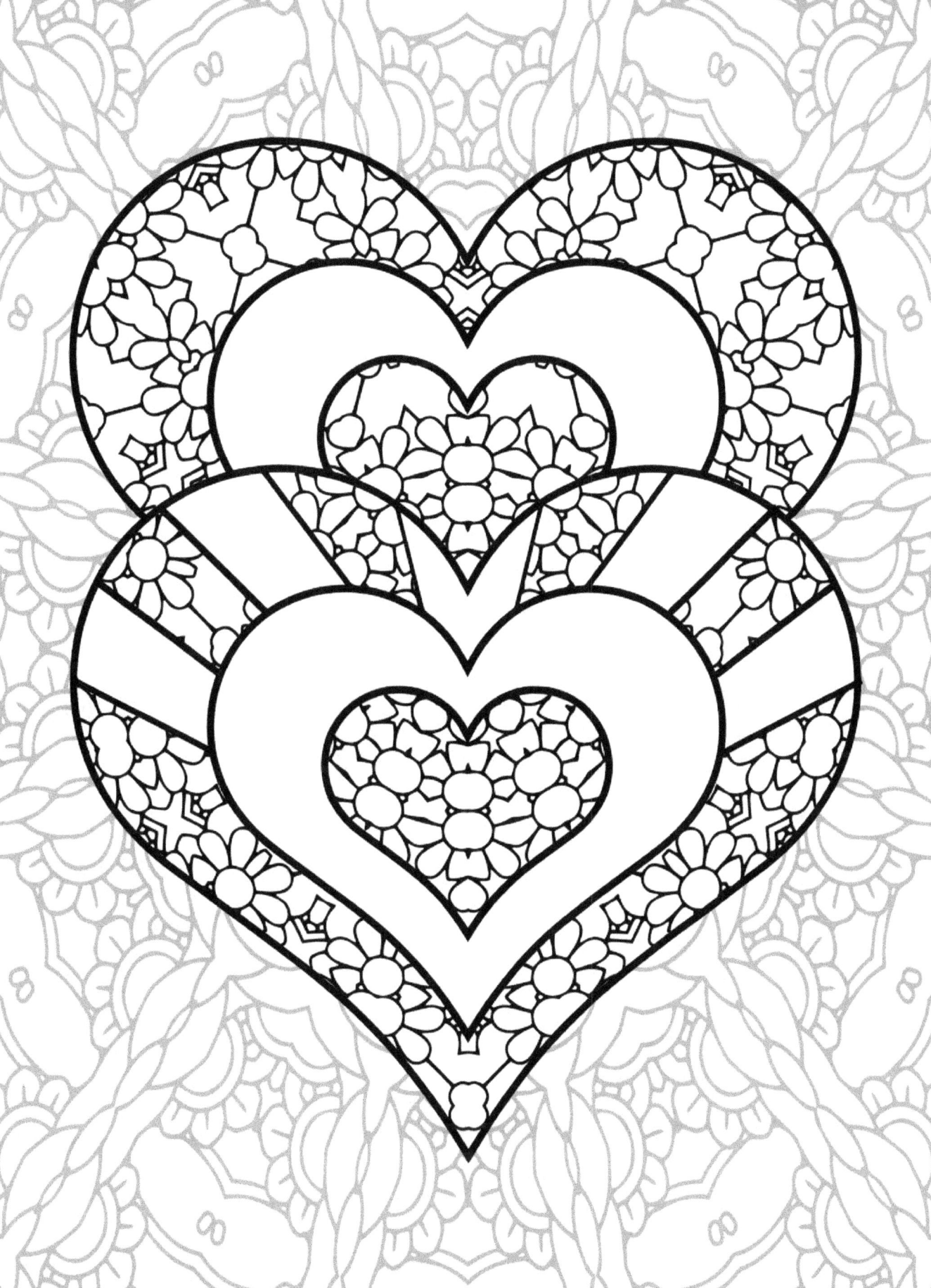

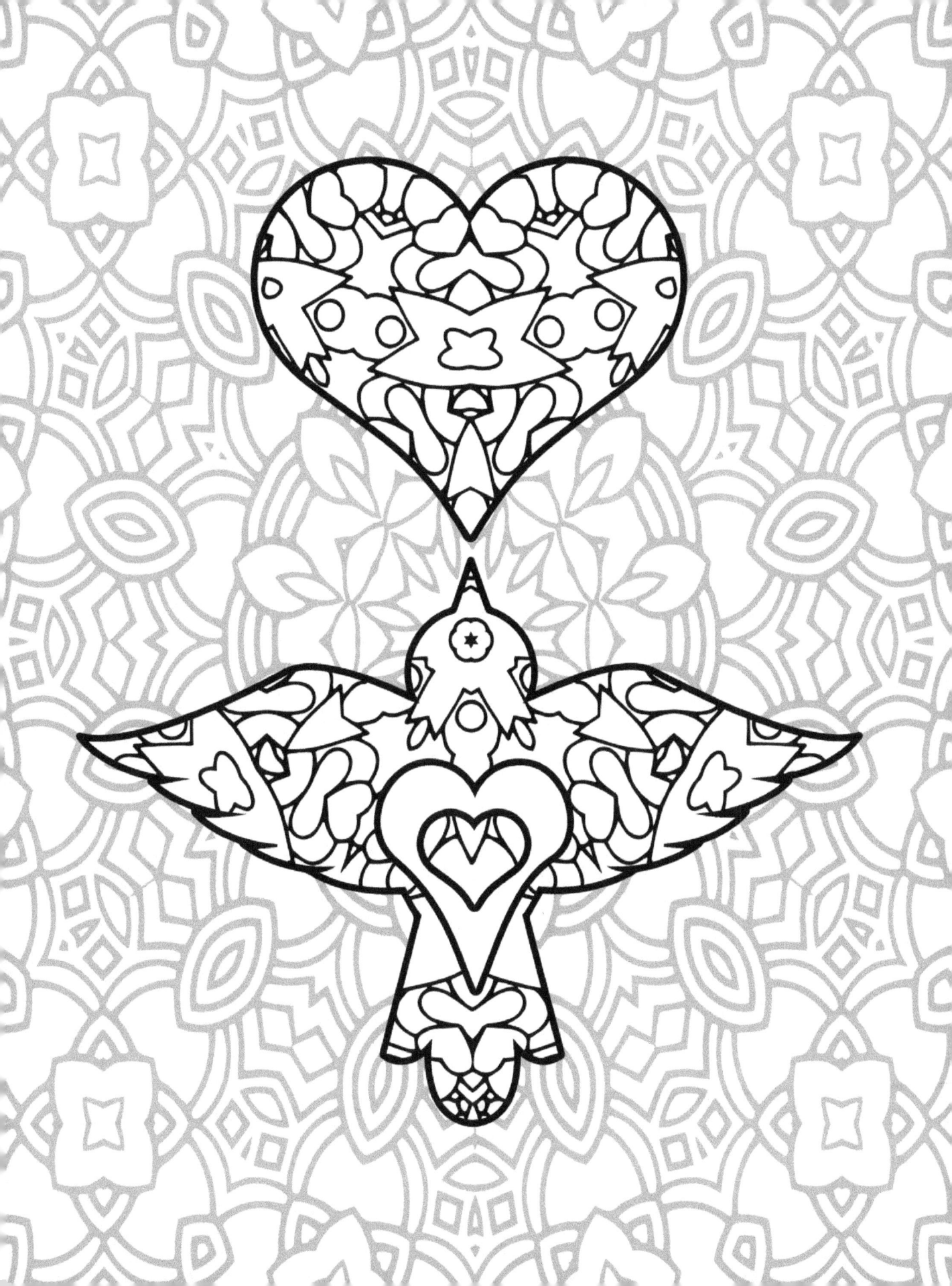

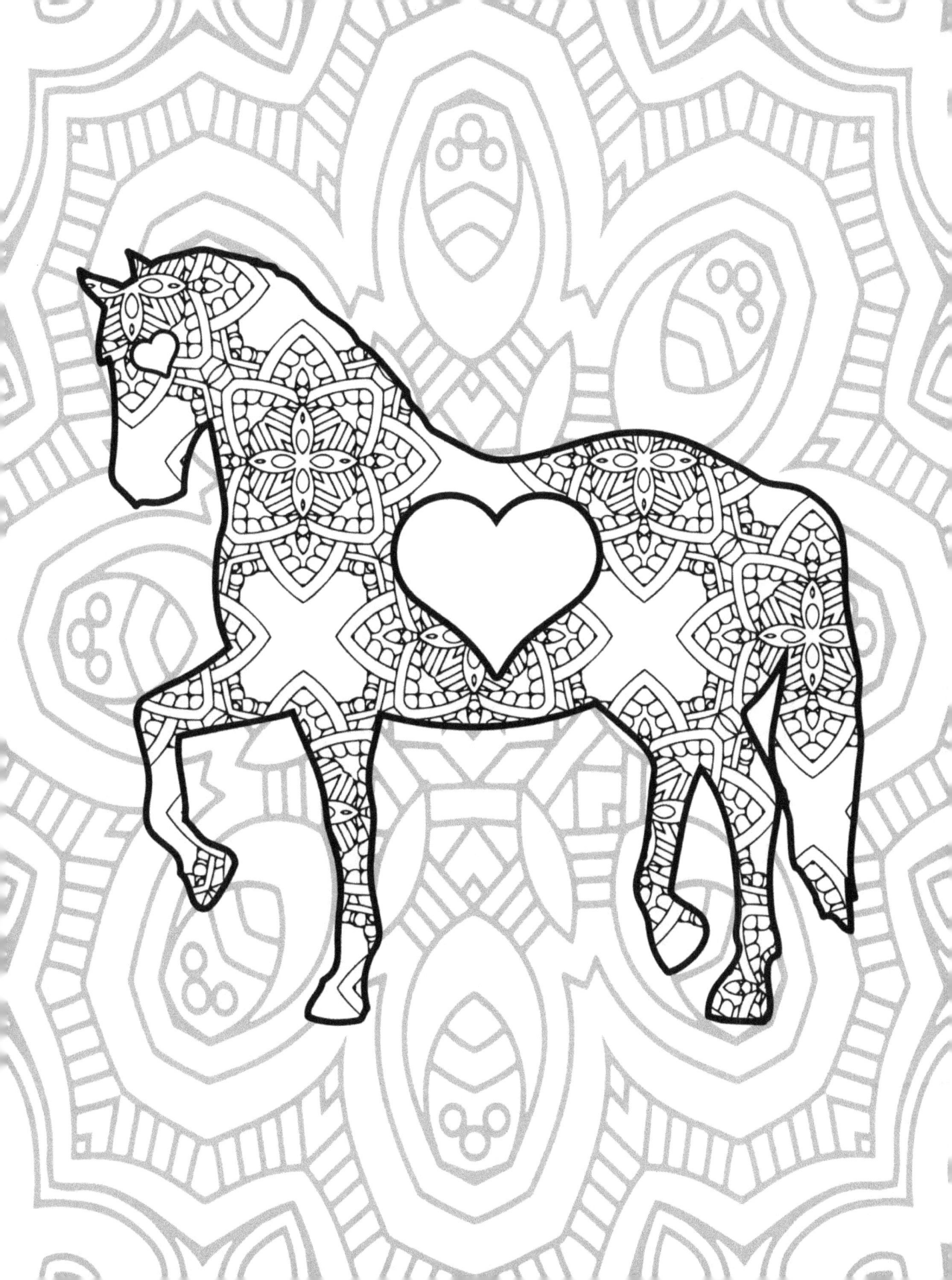

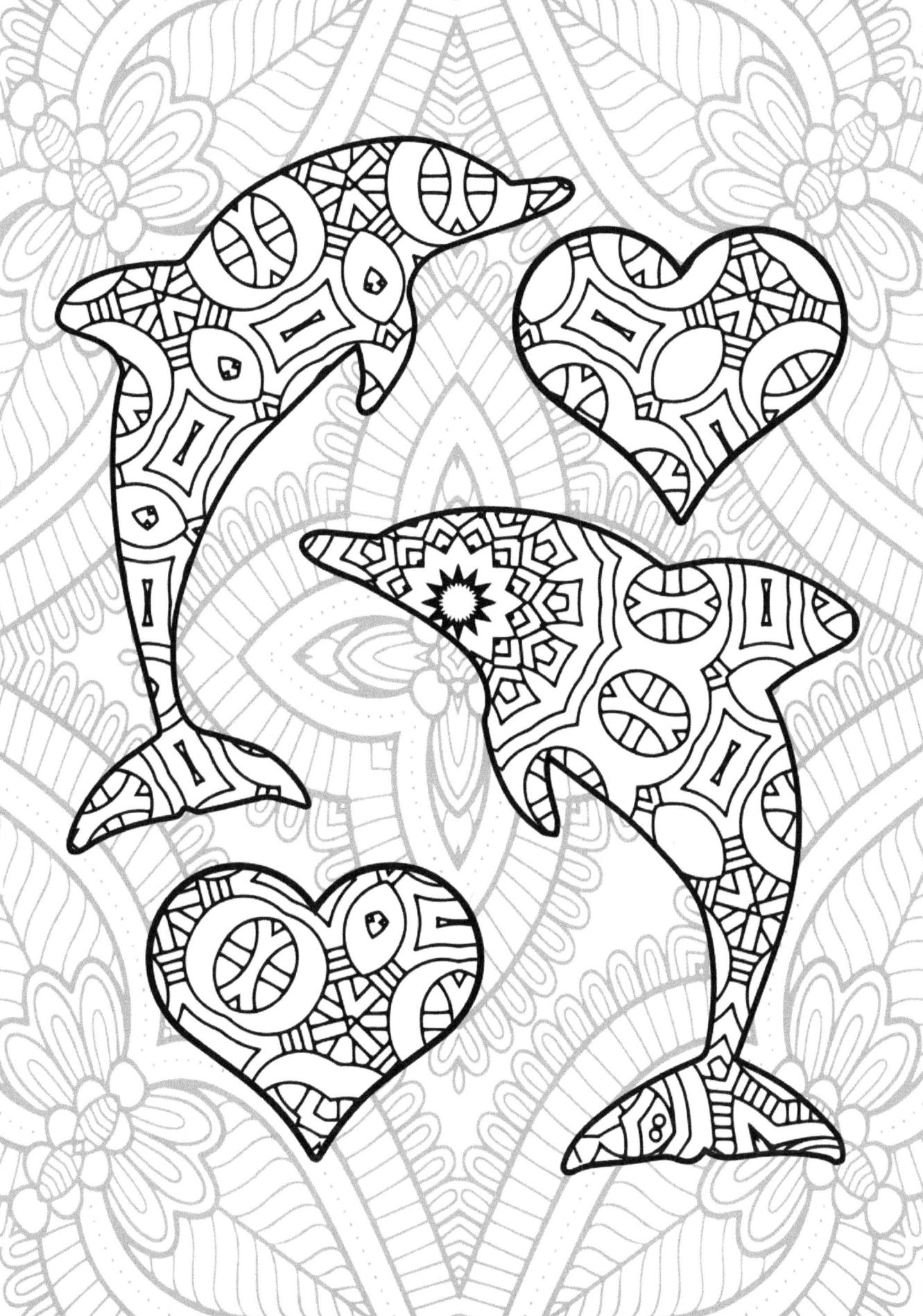

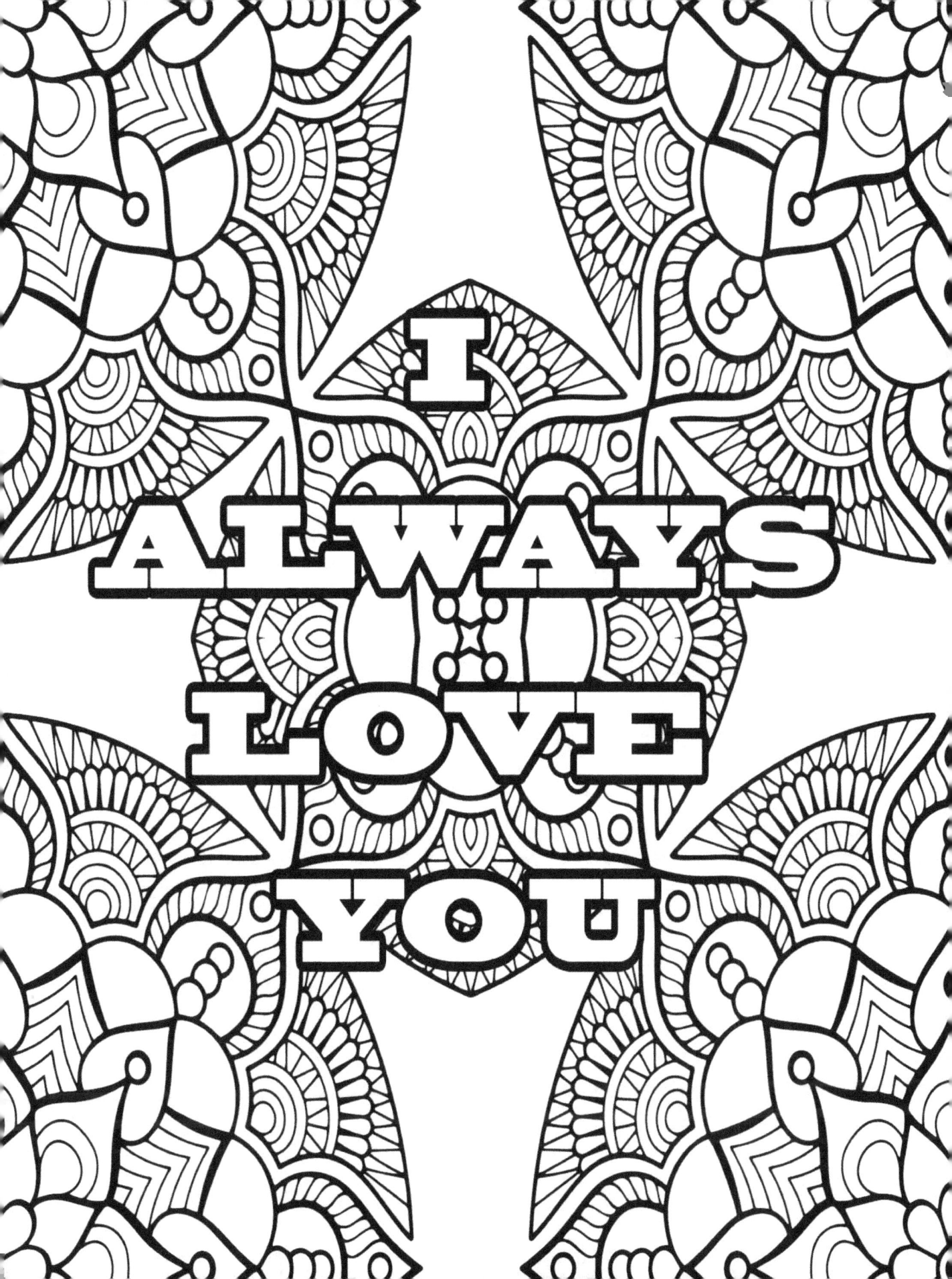

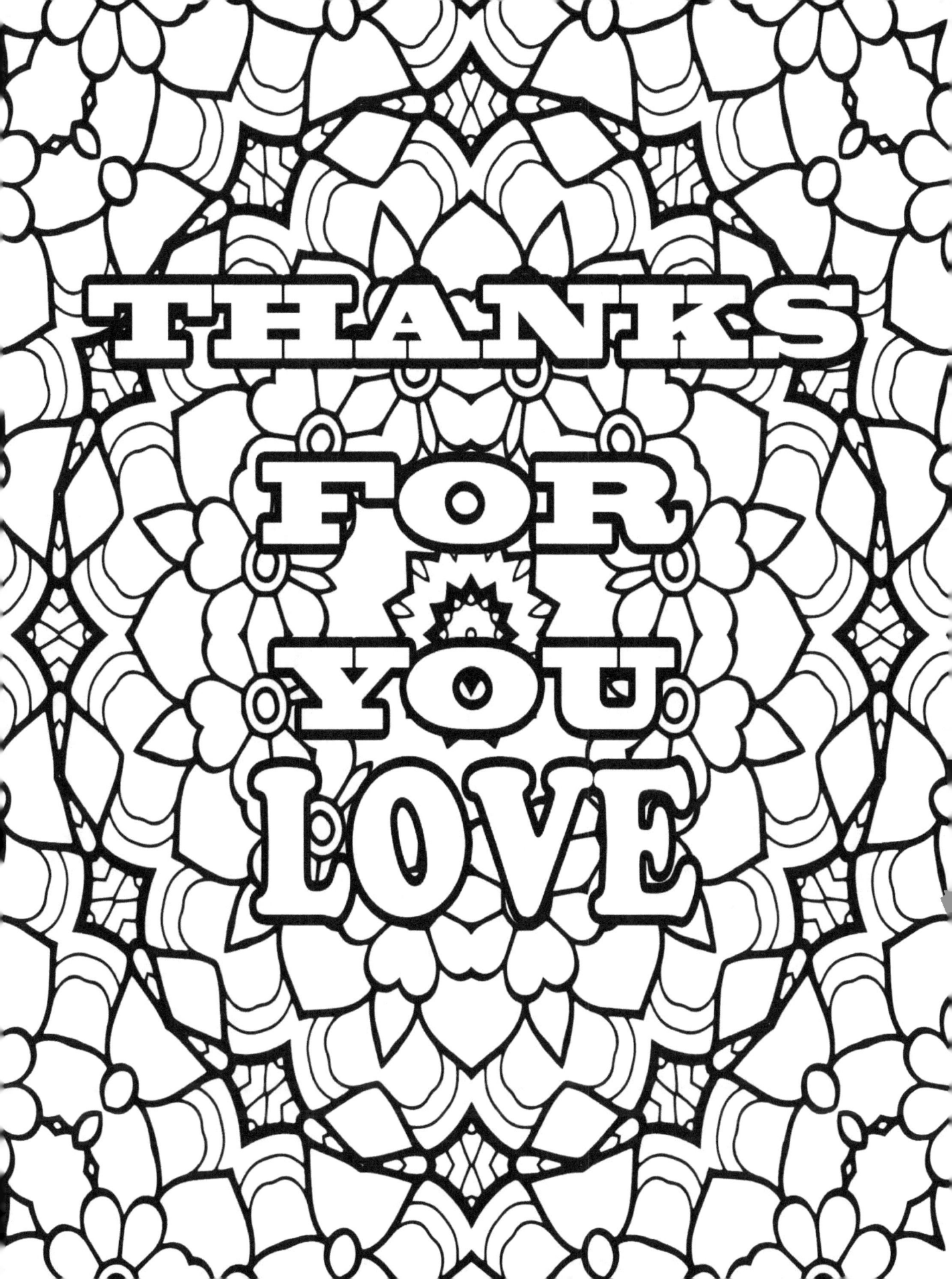

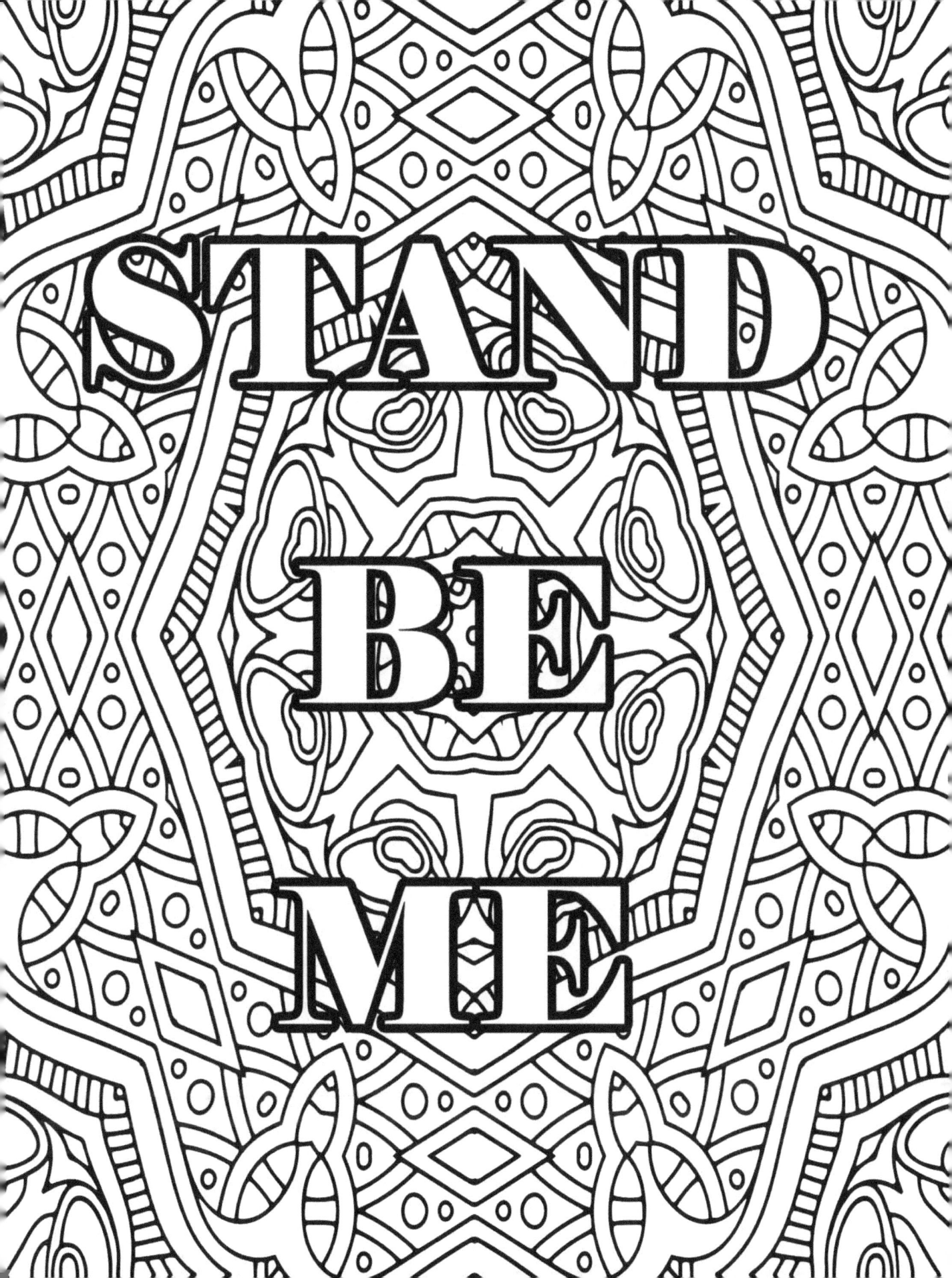

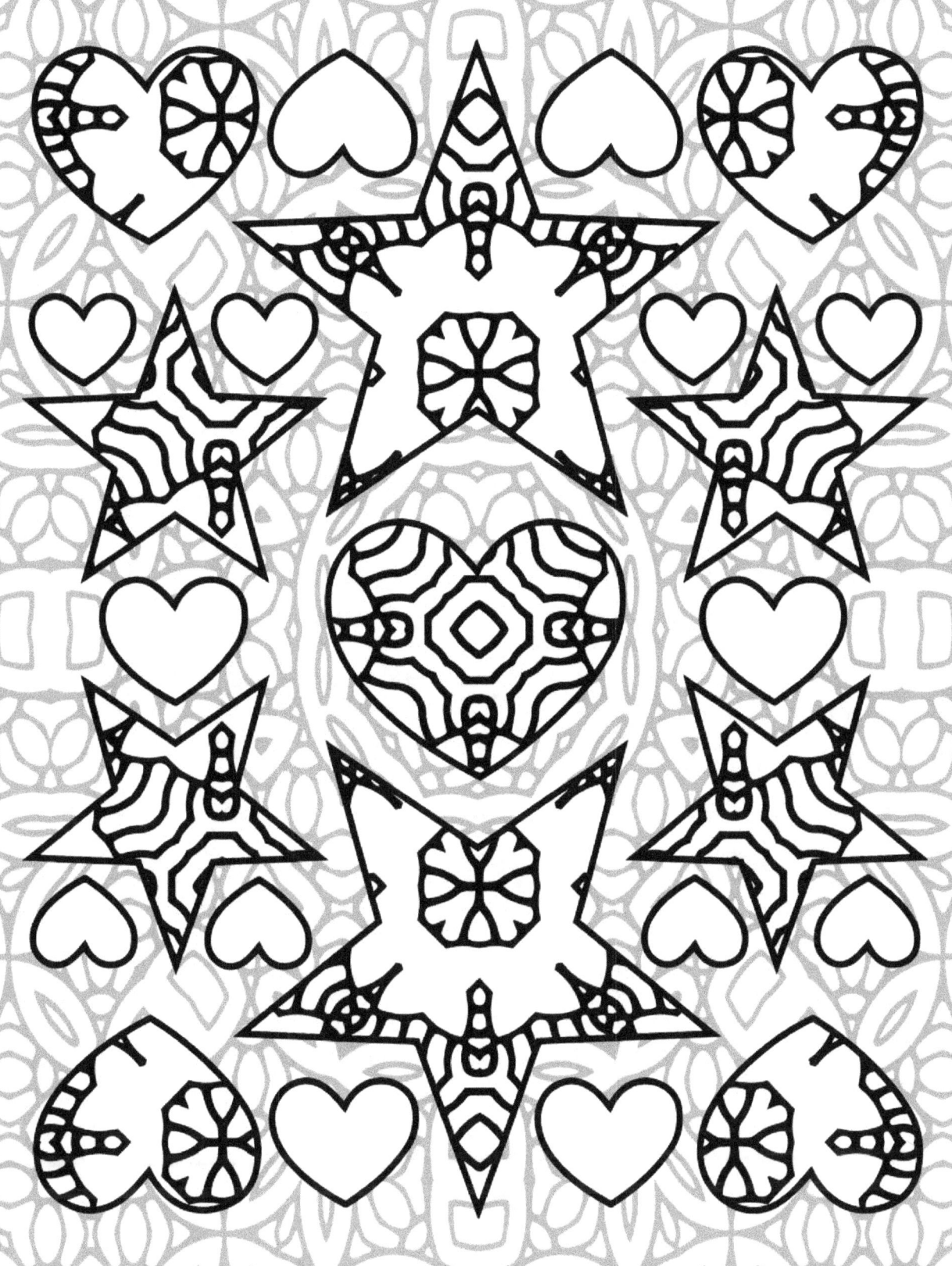

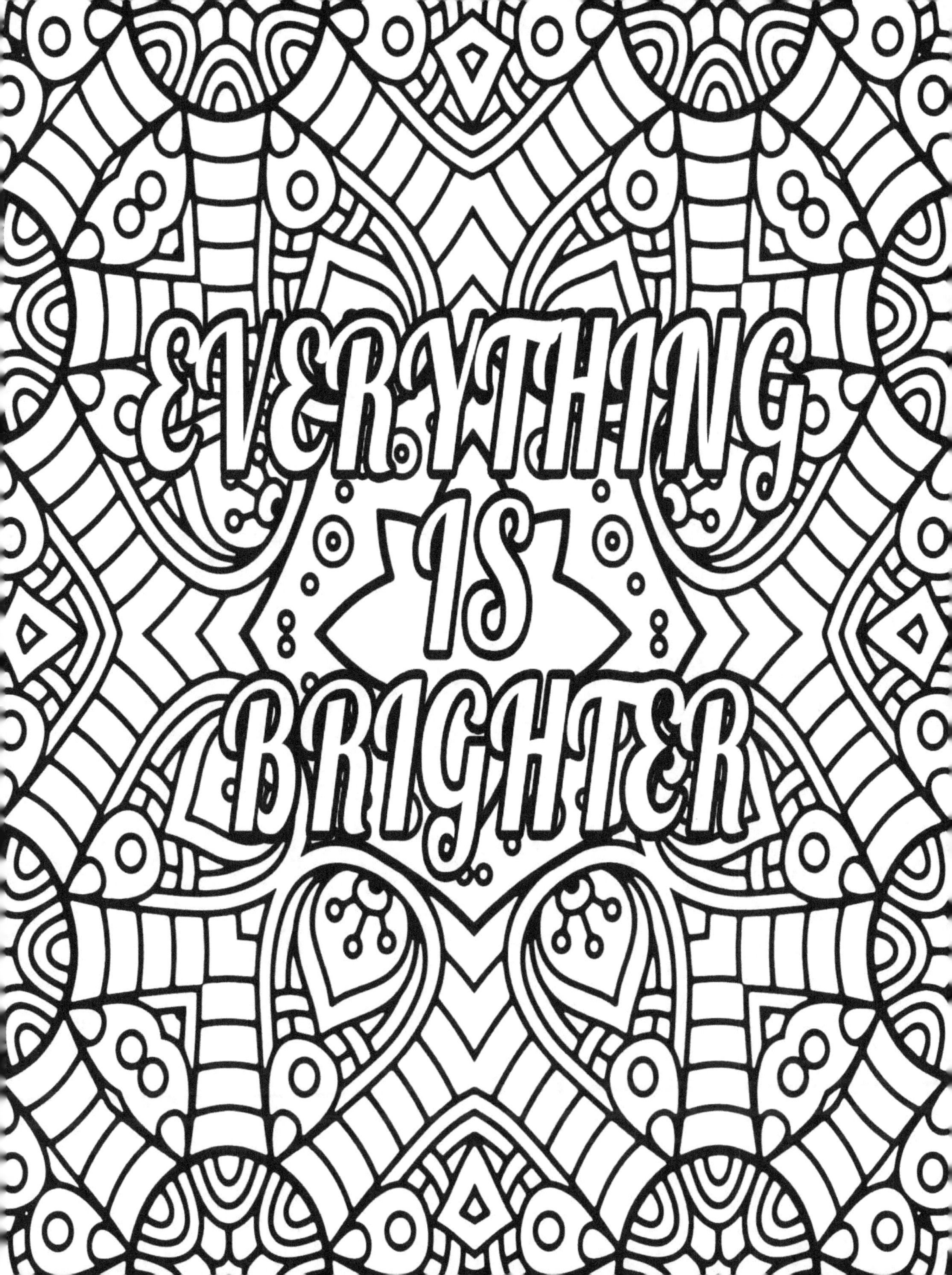

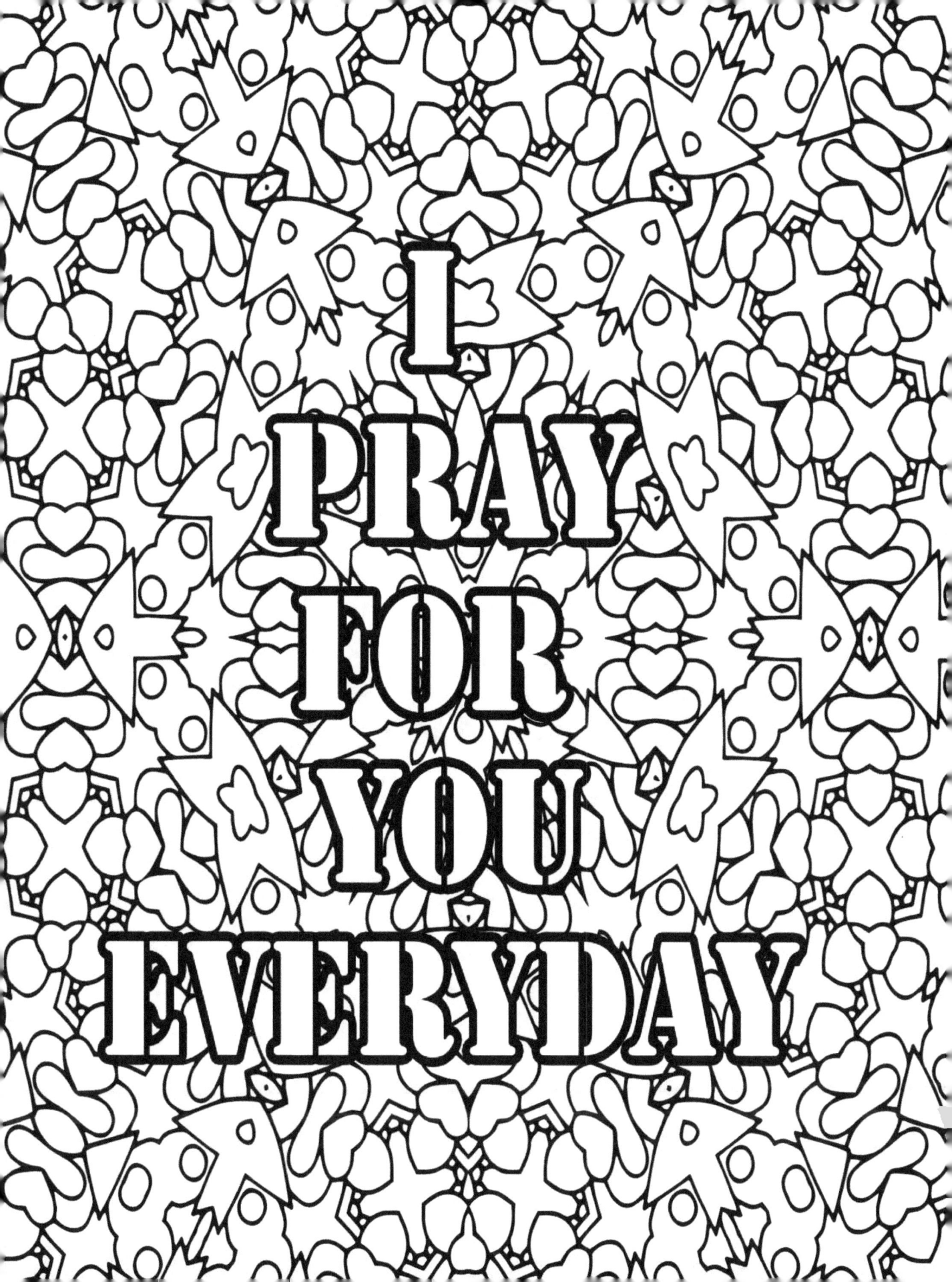

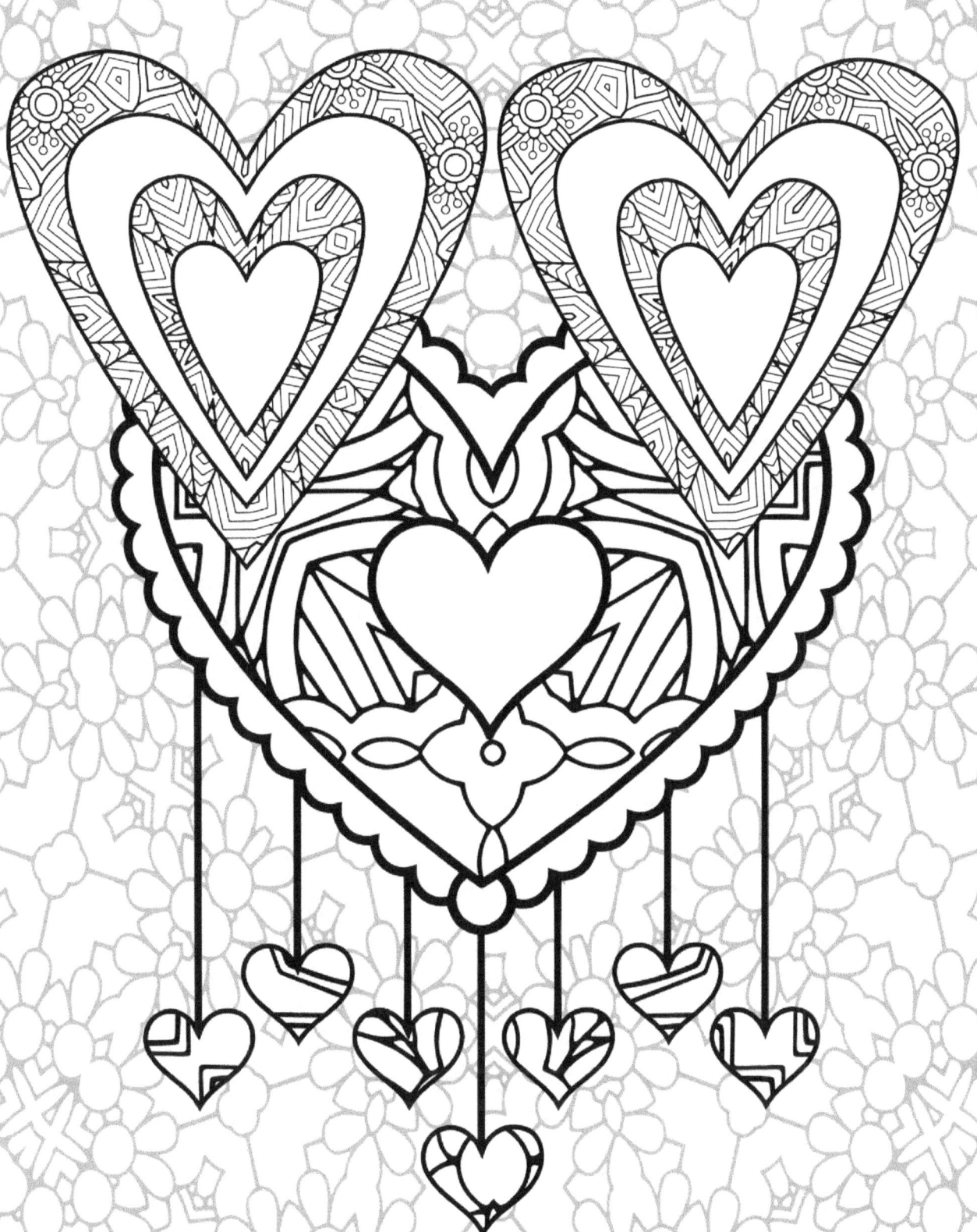

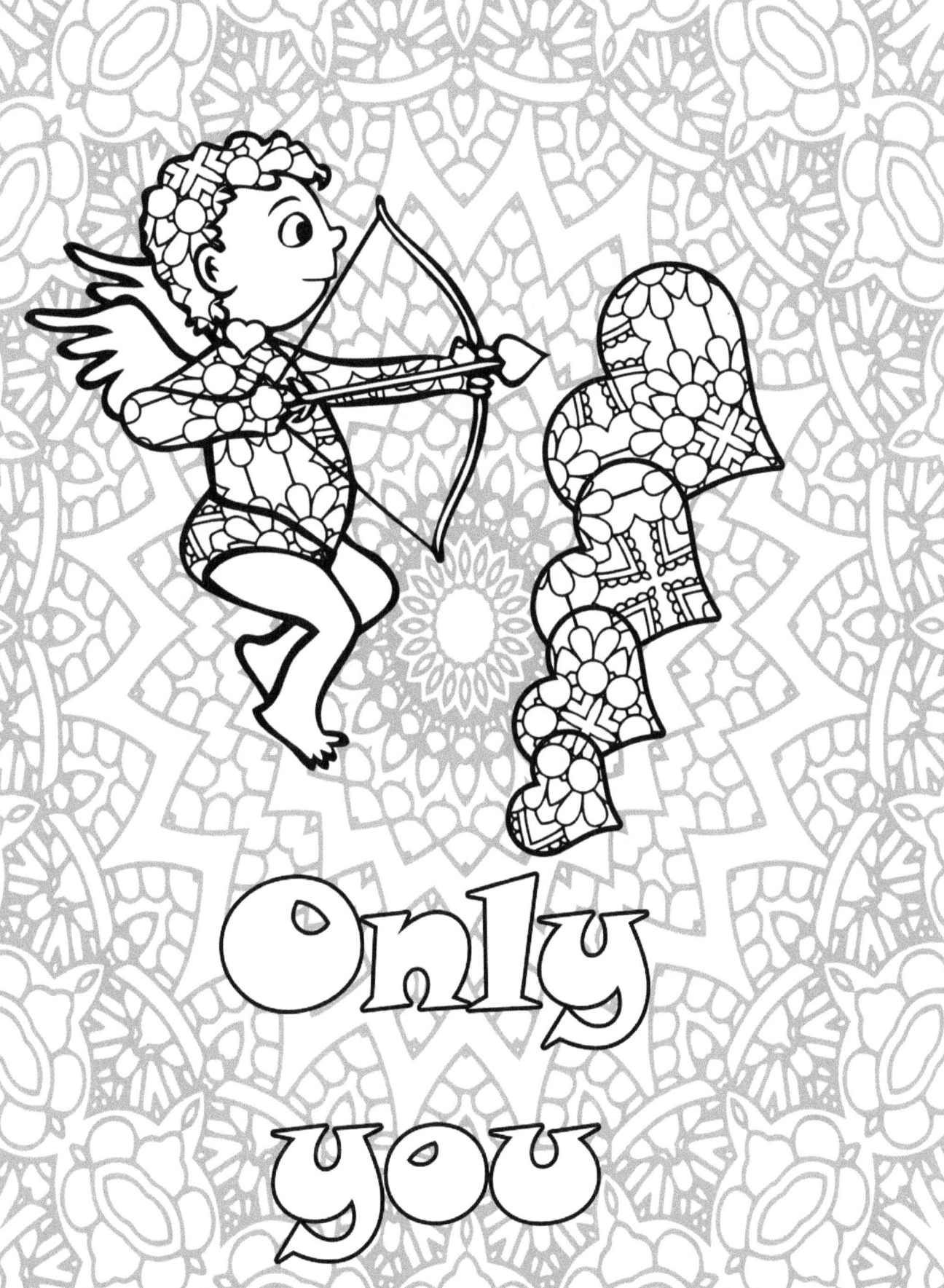

Visit
http://www.creatudiariosecreto.com/valent
ines
to have 5 exclusive pages to download and
print.

Other Publications

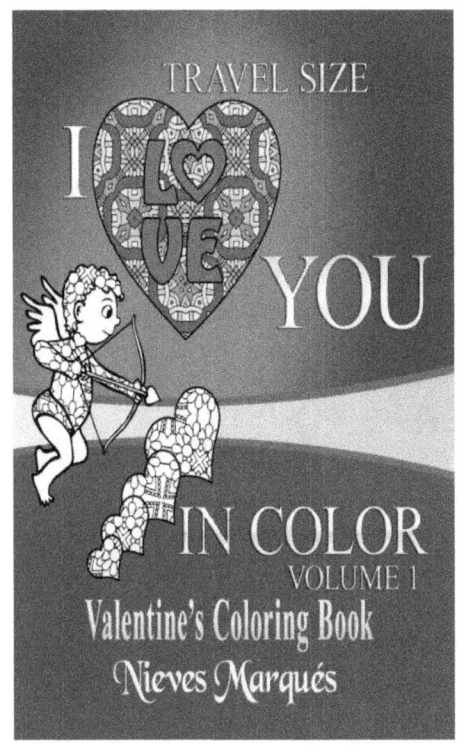

Crea tu Diario Secreto
Vol 1.

Ideas Creativas y Desarrollo Personal
Vol 1.

Nieves Marqués

Crea tu Diario Secreto
Vol 1.

A todo Color

Ideas Creativas y Desarrollo Personal
Vol 1.

Nieves Marqués

www.ingramcontent.com/pod-product-compliance
Lightning Source LLC
Chambersburg PA
CBHW080305180526
45167CB00006B/2671